RHODES
AND THE
HOLOCAUST

The Story of the Jewish Community from the Mediterranean Island of Rhodes

BASED ON ACTUAL EVENTS

ISAAC BENATAR

iUniverse, Inc.
New York Bloomington

Rhodes and the Holocaust

iUniverse books may be ordered through booksellers or by contacting:

iUniverse
1663 Liberty Drive
Bloomington, IN 47403
www.iuniverse.com
1-800-Authors (1-800-288-4677)

Because of the dynamic nature of the Internet, any Web addresses or links contained in this book may have changed since publication and may no longer be valid. The views expressed in this work are solely those of the author and do not necessarily reflect the views of the publisher, and the publisher hereby disclaims any responsibility for them.

ISBN: 978-1-4502-3451-1 (sc)
ISBN: 978-1-4502-3452-8 (hb)
ISBN: 978-1-4502-3453-5 (ebook)

Printed in the United States of America

iUniverse rev. date: 06/02/2010

This book is dedicated to the memory of my grandparents Isaac and Djoya Hanan, Allegra Hanan, and the innocent lives from "La Juderia" on the Island of Rhodes who became victims of the Nazis and the Holocaust.

Never Forget!

My thanks to all who contributed with their personal experiences and accounts of the events that unfolded on the Island of Rhodes. My special thanks to Aron Hasson and the Rhodes Jewish Historical Foundation for allowing me to reproduce and use photographs from its archives.

My thanks go to Suzanne Gurland Lazarus for proofing the final manuscript.

Contents

PREFACE

My maternal grandparents were killed as a result of the Nazi occupation on the Island of Rhodes. My grandmother and aunt perished while seeking shelter from falling bombs and my grandfather during his deportation to Auschwitz Concentration Camp.

While much of the focus of the accounts of the Holocaust refer to events as they affected the Jewish populations of Eastern and Middle Europe such as France, Poland, Hungary and Czechoslovakia, little seems to be widely known of events that took place in Greece and the surrounding Aegean Islands. Perhaps it is because their population was almost annihilated from a thriving community of over eighty thousand, to less than a thousand survivors to tell their stories.

This story tells of the events that befell the Jewish community known as "La Juderia" of Rhodes Island, the largest of the twelve Dodecanese islands in the Mediterranean Sea, near the coast of Turkey.

As a descendant of one of those families, with a heritage dating back several generations in La Juderia, I traveled to Rhodes in August 2007 to visit that island jewel. I went to the Jewish Quarter - once populated with a vibrant Jewish community, where my ancestors had lived. I visited the places where my parents were born, and had spent their youth. I went to the cemetery to pay my respects at the gravesites of my grandparents and aunt. I also made a daily pilgrimage to the "Shalom" synagogue the oldest and lone surviving temple of the Jewish Quarter.

While at the synagogue, I listened to a lecture given by one of the few survivors of the Holocaust from Rhodes Island. Now in his late seventies, he had only in the last few years opened up to talking publicly of how, as a thirteen year old boy, he had been taken to Auschwitz.

Tears flowed from my eyes as I listened to him tell of his life. His words painted a heart-wrenching picture of the events that befell La Juderia during World War Two. He told of the Nazi's rounding up the Jewish community, including himself, his eleven-year-old sister and his father. His narrative explained the deceit employed by the Nazis in the preparation, imprisonment and deportation of the entire Jewish community to a concentration camp. His voice pained as he related the inhuman treatment they experienced while being transported aboard cargo freighters to Greece, and by train to Auschwitz. He told of his experiences as a young boy at Auschwitz and of losing his father and eleven-year-old sister to the horrors of the camp. He described how the eventual "liberation" by the Russians left the survivors of the concentration camp abandoned to the mercy of the forces of nature during a brutally cold Polish winter. He told of his continued labor for the Russians even after the war had ended. He described his eventual escape from the Russians and of walking across Germany to freedom in Italy. He went on to start a new life as a merchant in Africa's Congo, but always carrying with him a burden - the memories of his experiences. He is one of the innocents who were victims of the concentration camps.

I stayed on the island for a further ten days and visited the synagogue daily. The survivor was always there and we got to converse on a regular basis in the Judeo-Spanish language, "Ladino". He was proficient in French and Italian, but spoke very little English.

During our conversations, he related to me that he had retired to Rome and spent the summer months in Rhodes lecturing on his experiences. He had been featured in the European television and newspaper media, which had carried stories of his horrifying experiences. He had become a public figure, and been honorably mentioned by the President of Italy. He wanted people to know of the horrifying events that had taken place. I explained to him that I was an author and presented my first book, "The Song of Africa", to the synagogue library. It contained a reference to my parents' heritage on the island.

With the revelation that I was an author, he placed his hand on my shoulder.

He said to me. "You should write the story of Rhodes!"

He clasped his hand over his heart as if taking something out of his chest and placed his hand over my heart as though transferring it to me.

"You are a descendant of the people of Rhodes. You would be able to tell the story with a special understanding. Write the story son, so that the world does not forget what happened here!"

I listened to his suggestion with an initial sense of reticence. In the past, I had difficulty in even viewing the Holocaust Museum in Washington DC, close to my home in Annapolis, Maryland. Now, he was asking me to write about those events. I pondered over the prospect and came to the realization that destiny had granted me a special reason for being at this place and time. It was the opportunity to write the story of a special people, where the words for the manuscript would flow from my heart. I decided to come to terms with the situation and concluded that irrespective of my own feelings of abhorrence to the Holocaust, it was a story that needed to be told. I determined that while I would devote more than a few chapters to this survivor's experiences, I also wanted to tell the story of my grandparents and the disposition of the people of La Juderia as they were affected by the events.

Returning home to the United States, I set all else aside. I had been writing another book, I had a small jewelry wholesale business and my regular job; all were sidelined, in order to devote time to this project.

For my research, I am appreciative for having resided amongst the large Sephardic community of Rhodesia, in Africa. Almost the entire generation of my parent's friends had been born on Rhodes Island and had immigrated to this new African country. I grew up listening to my parents and their friends talking about their lives on the island.

I am grateful to Aron Hasson, president of the Rhodes Holocaust Museum for his input, allowing me to reproduce and use photos from the museum and for the documentation relating to Giuseppe Cone. To John Redfern (retired Colonel), for sending me the documentation relating to his father, Captain Alan Redfern's planned clandestine mission to Rhodes. To Bernard Turiel for sharing his experiences as one of the "Turkish Jewish" families that survived the Holocaust deportations from Rhodes.

This is the story of the Jewish community of Rhodes Island and their struggle for survival

***

A Holocaust memorial is situated within the remains of the bombed-out square of the old city of Rhodes. An epitaph on the black marble monument is displayed in six languages. In English, it reads: "In eternal memory of the 1604 Jewish Martyrs of Rhodes and Cos who were murdered in Nazi death camps."

Of the few that survived nearly all were young boys and girls orphaned by the genocide.

***

CHAPTER 1

THE PRELUDE

Beautiful Rhodes is the largest of the Dodecanese cluster of islands nestled in the Mediterranean Sea. A mere stone's throw away, across a short span of the sea from the port, you can see the Western mountains of Turkey.

Rich in history and fabled Greek mythology, the tales of life on the island stretch back over four thousand years. Centuries ago, the port of Rhodes-boasted at its entrance one of the seven ancient wonders of the world- the Colossus of Rhodes.

The Order of the Knights Hospitaliers of Saint John of Jerusalem purchased the island in 1309. After defeats in Jerusalem and Cyprus, the Knights established Rhodes as their headquarters. During their two-hundred-year era, the fortifications were enlarged with the addition of several public buildings, including a hospital, palace and churches.

In 1522, after a long siege, the Ottoman Turks conquered the city from the Knights. New buildings, such as mosques and mansions, were added to the existing fortified castle walls.

Despite the conquests by the Ottoman Empire, and later, by the Italians and Germans, Rhodes is the most perfectly preserved and still functional medieval town and castle fortress in the world.

In late fifteenth-century Spain, the merciless Inquisition, combined with the Alhambra Edicts of Queen Isabella and King Ferdinand of Spain, ushered in a period of terror for the Spanish Jews, known as Sephardim. Finally, expelled from their homes and property, they set sail in search of a new home. The Ottoman Muslims welcomed them to settle in Rhodes in the sixteenth century.

Earlier, there had been a minor presence of Jews on the island starting back two thousand years. However, with the arrival of the expelled Spanish community, there became established La Juderia, the Jewish quarter in the old fortress city of Rhodes. It was located in the eastern portion of the castle fortress, near a pier used by the large ships. The society became centered surrounding the street where the Kahal Gadol synagogue existed. In time, three more synagogues would be erected. The community grew and flourished under the Turks.

Italian troops captured Rhodes and the Dodecanese in 1912 and later in 1923 established the colony "Isole Italiane Del Egeo".

By 1918, the Jewish community of La Juderia had grown to over 4,000. Many of the customs and traditions brought from Spain by their ancestors to the island continued to be handed down and observed through the generations. While most were multi-lingual in Greek, Italian, French and Turkish, the common language within the society was a Judeo-Spanish dialect known as Ladino. The Ladino language through time had become so ingrained on the island that some of the Greek and Turkish friends had also learned and were able to converse in that dialect during their social interactions with members of the Jewish community.

There was a very solid sense of affiliation within La Juderia, with its basis in religion, customs, and tradition; a combination that translated into a charming, warm and collective familial way of life. The closeness of the society was often reflected during conversations, where in speech older women often referred to each other with the respectful prefix of "hermana" translating from Ladino into "sister". Typical of a greeting between the women would be;

"Ke haber, Hermana Esther?" - "How are you, Sister Esther?"

The men were involved in all aspects of society; they were professionals, bankers, merchants, religious students and regular employees. While the synagogue was the societal center of their lives, interactions with the other ethnic groups on the island were on a secular level. Some wonderful friendships had developed and thrived amongst the people of La Juderia and their Greek and Turkish neighbors.

The vast castle fortress with its medieval stone walls surrounding the Jewish quarter resembled in many ways the structures of the walled fortress city in the holy land. That aspect, earned La Juderia the affectionate tag of "Little Jerusalem" by its inhabitants.

Many in La Juderia had done very well, such as the Alhadeff family who had become wealthy bankers and merchants. As in any society, some had not had such a measure of success, like Isaac and Djoya Hanan. Isaac was a poor mattress maker with a family of nine children. They lived in a one-bedroom house, a short distance from the synagogue in Dossiadou Street. Often, they were unable to make ends meet and survived in their cramped space on the barest of essentials. Although poor by any standards, they were a happy family and the children were all gifted in one way or another. At age thirteen, the eldest son Morris set off by boat for the United States to start a new life and a quest to make his fortune. The second eldest son, Leon, quit school at age eleven to work, and also left for America to find employment that would enable him to send back money to support the family. The eldest of the daughters, Serena, helped her parents by doing odd jobs, the household chores, and bringing up her sisters and brothers. The fourth child, Mathilda, at the age of five, was given to more wealthy relatives as an "esclava" – an unpaid servant, to make ends meet.

The middle child, Rachel, had the gift of intelligence. She had graduated from high school at the age of twelve and by age fourteen was a schoolteacher of pupils older than herself. She taught at the Alliance Israelite Universelle, the school of La Juderia.

After completing her teaching at the Alliance, Rachel often loaded an old satchel with papers from her students that needed to be graded. She would set off to find a spot to mark their work. Walking a short distance along the narrow and winding streets, she would pass houses brimming with life. Familiar and smiling faces of families outside their time worn steps and through the alleyways, greeted her along her route. Her home was a short distance from the school, but she would keep walking towards the street of "La Calle Ancha" – the wide street and adjacent "Tcharshi" business district where many merchants exhibited their wares. Rachel's earnings were used to help support her family. She knew that she could not afford to purchase any of the items the street so beautifully displayed, but still took pleasure at the window-shopping.

Merchants and shoppers bustled with activity, greeting each other in Ladino the Judeo-Spanish language, Greek and Turkish. Occasionally, a dash of other languages would also permeate into the exchanges. Young Turkish men, some still clad in the old traditional Shalvars, a dress of baggy pants, busily worked at the outdoor restaurants serving coffee, wine and Raki liquor.

Beyond the merchants' shops, Rachel walked by the Grand Masters' Palace, a vast stone castle where the former rulers of the island had presided over Rhodes. Finally, she would reach the outermost stone arches of the medieval city's walls and exit the castle to head towards her goal, the Mandraki, the port situated on the Western end of the city fortifications.

At the port, fishing boats had begun returning into the harbor carrying their trawling catches and the air carried a strong aroma of fish. Alongside the docks, a few boats were already moored with men working on repairing their fishnets and scrubbing the decks from the day's fishing venture. The vista at this site was impressively enhanced by the presence of three large medieval stone windmills. The structures stood as magnificent backdrops to the port and Mediterranean Sea beyond. On the western side of the port lay a beautiful pebbled beach dotted with people sunbathing and swimming amongst the gentle incoming waves.

Rachel would make her way behind the central windmill and settle herself comfortably on the rocks facing the sea. This tranquil spot was her private place to enjoy the surroundings and to work marking her students' papers. On occasion, she would take a break from the paperwork and gaze with concern across the blue waters of the Mediterranean. She thought about the new Italian rulers of the island. Life had been good under their influence. They had built a new city outside the old fortified walls and had improved the amenities on the island. The governing Italian inhabitants seemed to be pleasant and reasonable people, but the decrees regularly issued by their Roman autocrats were often harsh. There was also a rising tide of Fascism in Italy and she shuddered, wondering if her beloved community was entering into a new era of persecution.

Returning home, Rachel would usually find three of her younger siblings playing in the narrow street outside their home. Each was two years apart in age. Rita was the next in line and widely considered the prettiest girl on the island. Next was Raphael, with a wonderful sense of humor and then Salvatore, with his shy, gentle personality.

The youngest of all the siblings, Allegra, was still a few-months -old baby, and remained in their mother's care.

Rachel and her siblings would smell the enticing aroma of appetizing herbs and spices wafting from their mother's cooking and that of surrounding neighbors' kitchens. With fair regularity, almost every day seemed to have a reason for a feast. The birth of a child, a Bar mitzvah, a new engagement, a wedding, the Sabbath and of course, the Jewish festivals – all were enjoyed equally with food delicacies, whether one was rich or poor.

Inside the small home, their mother Djoya would be working hard over the wood stove on a platter of pastries that had sent out those appealing delicate wafts. She was a kindly and warm person. Somehow, despite the large size of her family, she always found time to give each of her children her tender full care and attention. Later in the evening, their father, Isaac, would arrive home from his hard day's labor. The children would crowd around him calling out the affectionate and respectful name "Signor" as each vied for his attention.

The horrifying events of the First World War had recently come to finality. Rhodes was largely untouched by the fighting, but at the end of the war in 1918, the economies of the whole of Europe were devastated. Many of the younger generation affected by the austerity, began to emigrate in the hopes of garnering a living in a new country. When conditions improved, some hoped to return to Rhodes one day.

Most were attracted by the allure of a new life in America and set off for cities such as New York, Los Angeles, and Seattle. Others had become fascinated by the adventures of Solomon and Gabrielle Benatar. The two had settled in brand new lands, which only a few years earlier had been part of uncharted darkest Africa. Those émigrés embarked for the new wilderness countries of Rhodesia and the Congo.

Rachel's older brothers began to send money back to Rhodes to help support the family and to assist the older siblings to come to America. By 1921, Serena, then Mathilda and the younger sister Rita, had left for the United States. Rachel had also received money to assist her with passage to the new land. However, she had delayed leaving and stayed behind with the remaining three younger siblings to assist with their care. Quietly, she placed the money sent to her into her parents money savings tin, secreted in their tiny pantry.

The following year in 1922, Rachel was courted by Victor Benatar, a Jewish youth in his early twenties from Rhodes. The eldest of three brothers, he was a tall, handsome, and an athletic young man. His parents were respected import merchants on the island. After a few months, they became engaged to be married. The same year, Benito Mussolini and his fascist regime came into power in Italy.

The decrees of "Il Duce," the widespread slang name given to the fascist leader Mussolini, were dispatched. They contained several restrictions on activities within Italian jurisdiction, making life harder for the people of Rhodes as a whole. Rumors were rife that soon more edicts were to be promulgated to enforce the autocratic fascist agenda

Rachel's fiancé called at her home one evening in late 1922. On this occasion, she sensed from the serious expression on his face, that he had something important on his mind. Victor requested that they take their evening stroll towards the eastern pier a few hundred yards from Rachel's home. As they ambled along the winding narrow streets and reached the fortress's stone arched door to the sea, the outlet known as "Puerto del Mar", Victor took her hand and gently held it in his. He turned to her, saying that he wanted to talk about their future together. Rachel nervously, took in a deep breath, in anticipation of what he wanted to discuss with her.

Victor began to explain that the economic hardships experienced on the island were having a negative effect on his father's import trade. His father had as a consequence decided to wind down and close the business. His father in a few months would be leaving with Victor's youngest brother for the opportunities opening up in Africa. Victor wanted the couple to join his father so that they could start their new life together under conditions that offered a greater opportunity for them. He told Rachel that he hoped that once economic conditions improved on Rhodes they would be able to return and continue life in their land of birth. His mother was going to remain behind in the island, on that expectation.

Rachel understood what Victor was telling her. She too, had doubts of their future prospects in the island. She agreed to start their new life in Africa.

It was not easy telling Rachel's parents of the decision, but they understood and gave the young couple their blessings. Surprisingly, her two younger brothers told Rachel that they too had been exploring the opportunities of traveling to either America or Africa. Rachel and Victor's decision to go to Africa weighed heavily with their final selection. They too, would join them and travel to Africa.

When the fateful day arrived, Isaac and Djoya walked the short distance from their home to the eastern pier to say farewell to Rachel and her brothers. Allegra, their youngest, and now the only remaining child, was now five years old. She walked in the middle tightly clasping the hands of both her mother and father. Sadly, they stood below the freighter ship, while Rachel and her brothers prepared to board for their voyage to Africa. With hugs and kisses, they parted.

Standing by the ships' railings, Rachel and her fiancé Victor, accompanied by Raphael and Salvotore, stood waving farewell as the boat pulled away from the harbor. Unknowingly, their exodus would save them from the impact of the rise of Italian Fascism and the German Holocaust.

Isaac and Djoya remained standing at the pier as the ship embarked and stayed watching, as the boat became a distant speck on the horizon.

Allegra looked up through her tear-filled eyes at her parents. She saw the anguish and sadness on their faces as they watched their children go. Looking back at the tiny speck on the horizon, Allegra silently made a promise to herself that she would never leave the island and her parents.

Slowly, the three walked thoughtfully and silently the short distance back to the house. Suddenly, their small one bedroom-home on Dossiadou Street appeared strangely spacious.

CHAPTER 2

FASCISM GAINS POWER

Over the next few years Benito Mussolini, "Il Duce," and his regime invoked their fascist agenda throughout Italy and its territories. Their policies were based on the myth of a national and racial rebirth - where the interests of individuals and races were subjugated to the national interest. The fascist leader appointed himself the authoritarian judge of what those interests would be.

Il Duce made personal visits to Rhodes to witness the decrees promulgated were being fully enforced. During the course of which, he turned the Grand Masters' Palace into a summer residence for himself. Having struck an alliance with Adolph Hitler, the Chancellor of Germany, a rising blend of Fascism and Nazism started to sprout.

The appointment of a Fascist Governor to the island with the power of passing autocratic decrees saw the gradual introduction of racial laws. While each passing edict became harsher, life for the populace of Rhodes and the community of La Juderia still remained good. Jewish inhabitants were subjected to subtle, but not yet severely harmful, targeting.

In 1936, the Governor, Conte Mario de Vecchi di Val Cismon, declared that the existing Jewish and Muslim cemeteries adjacent to the old city were to become "green zones". The bodies buried in those hallowed grounds over several centuries had to be removed and interred in a new place outside the city walls and further away from the old city. That year also saw the initial publication of a racial manifesto in Italy by Mussolini. Travel documents and passports became harder to obtain and the hopes of those wishing to leave and find a freer life, diminished.

Allegra had stayed true to her childhood promise of remaining in the island with her parents. With the passage of time, she had blossomed, and by 1937 was a beautiful young woman of nineteen. She had acquired natural good looks with smooth peaches and cream skin, brown smiling eyes and silky auburn, shoulder length hair. Her attractiveness was augmented by a charismatic smile that combined with a sensitive and warm personality. Affected by the era of the great depression, her brothers and sisters had only been able to send an occasional small amount from abroad to assist the family. She had obtained work as a receptionist at the Italian military offices in the new quarter of the city. She had also been able to bring some extra income to help her parents by doing after hour's jobs as they became available. Such work included cleaning at the officers' mess in the Italian military section. While performing her work at the mess, she occasionally overheard the sentiments voiced in conversations within the Italian military personnel. Allegra began to sense that many of them were becoming reluctant participants in the harsh rules and the regime they were supposed to enforce.

Allegra was not aware that one of the officers at the post, a handsome, tall, dark haired and olive tanned young lieutenant by the name of Vittorio, had taken a fancy to her. He had kept a watchful eye at the mess and had been quick to reprimand any of his men who had attempted to bother or harass the young girl. He had on occasion "accidentally" been out on the street late at night when Allegra came out from her work duties and volunteered his assistance to her.

"Buona sera, signorina Allegra, may I escort you safely home?"

At first, Allegra had naively interpreted Vittorio's behavior as that of an officer and a gentleman. She had appreciatively responded with a shy, "thank you, you are very kind, signore."

During those walks to Allegra's home, Vittorio had always kept the conversation light and casual without revealing his true affections for her. However, after a couple more occasions of the "coincidental" nightly encounters, Allegra began to understand that there was more to Vittorio's intentions.

One of Allegra's best girlfriends, Sarah, was about to be married, and such an occasion was always regarded as a special event by the community. It was an "open invitation" for the entire La Juderia to become involved and participate in the festivities.

Allegra was invited by her friend to be the maid-of-honor at the wedding. Since the process needed a lot of organization, her friend often joined Allegra at the military office during the lunch break to discuss the arrangements. Vittorio, from his nearby desk, would watch the two girls laughing and talking in their exchanges about the plans for the wedding. He felt his heart flutter briefly as he watched Allegra's smiling eyes and excited chatter with her friend. To the girls' surprise, the officer had on occasion joined their conversation and volunteered helpful suggestions.

Everyone in La Juderia, despite their limited means, contributed towards making the wedding a special celebration. For a few days, almost any harshness of life was forgotten. Women gathered in a communal catering area with assorted baking ingredients and cooked traditional cakes, pastries, and created sweets from fruit; called dulcies. The exquisite food was set out in trays and the women sang as they prepared the edibles. Laughter and jokes filled the previously somber air.

Almost all the inhabitants of La Juderia turned out to line the streets and join in the happiness for the "Banyu de novia" the procession of the bridal bath. Many of the Turkish and Greek neighbors also attended and contributed to the festive occasion. The bride and her trousseau were paraded along the lined streets and were met with singing and clapping along the route to her fiancé's house. Families living along the bridal route stood out on their second floor balconies to applaud the joyful procession.

As a bridesmaid, Allegra was in the center of the festivities. It was one of the happiest days of her life as she sang and danced along with the crowd. Isaac and Djoya watched with pride as they stood amongst the revelers and saw their daughter pass them performing the traditional dances within the wedding procession.

From a balcony café above the Calle Ancha, another admirer of Allegra, lieutenant Vittorio, watched the ongoing festivities as he sipped black Turkish coffee from a small cup. The view from the café offered a clear picture of the activities going on. As the officer returned his gaze to stare into the darkness inside of his cup, a sigh pursed through his lips. He was aware of the brevity of such happy occasions and that the performance of his new authoritarian instructions would ensure such briefness.

Allegra's brothers and sisters had always stayed in contact with her parents and her through their letters. The most regular of the writers was Rachel, with news of her family and brothers in their new land.

Rachel and Victor had settled in the British colony of Southern Rhodesia, in Africa, and now had two children. They, with her two brothers had carved out a farming venture in the previously wilderness land. While they enjoyed an existence without persecution and restrictions, life was not without perils in the new country. Malaria and Black Water Fever were rampant and claimed the lives of Victor's father and their youngest brother, Salvotore.

The couple was able to obtain British passports and returned with their children for a brief visit to Rhodes in 1937. There was a great deal of happiness at being united with their families and friends once more. At a combined dinner of the families during their visit, Victor made a toast. He told the family reunion that it was like "tasting the sweet nectar of honey" to be amongst them again on the island.

While they had a wonderful time together, Rachel and Victor were concerned about the rising tide of Mussolini's Fascism and the racial laws that accompanied that policy. They attempted to convince their respective families to return with them to Africa. Rachel's parents had gratefully responded to the young couple's appeals that they did not wish to be a burden on their children. They were now well into their sixties and believed it to be a little late to start life afresh. Allegra wished to remain on the island with her parents. They did however, succeed in convincing Victor's now widowed mother, Esther, to accompany them back to Africa to live with the family.

Rachel and her family departed from Rhodes for their journey back to Africa with sadness and heavy hearts for those they were leaving behind.

The following year, in July of 1938, the fascist "Manifesto degli Scienziati Razzisti" - Manifesto of the Racial Scientists, was adopted into law in Italy and throughout its territories. Fascism declared itself clearly anti-Semite. The racist laws contained in the document in reality had ninety percent of its contents authored by Mussolini, but purported to have been findings written by a group of scientists. Many believed it was the product of the Italian-German alliance.

The law declared the Italians to be descendants of the Aryan race, and it targeted races that were seen as inferior - those not of Aryan descent. In particular, Jews were banned from many professions. Under the racial laws, marriages between Italians and Jews were prohibited or dissolved, Jews were banned from positions in banking, government, and education and their properties were subject to confiscation.

The laws were strictly enforced. They had a wide-ranging effect on the lives of the community of La Juderia. Allegra, amongst others, lost her government job, while girls attending the Italian school of the nuns were no longer allowed to continue their education there. Professionals had to turn to other means, sometimes to menial jobs, to survive.

Allegra, through the assistance of Lieutenant Vittorio, was able to carry on with her part time work and earned some income from cleaning tasks at the officers' mess.

The clouds of war were looming over Europe. In the countries surrounding Rhodes, their leaders were positioning themselves with methodical chess-like moves to achieve or protect their desired interests. Il Duce began to eye nearby Greece with belligerence as being within Italy's sphere of domination. Turkey, on the other hand, while Axis friendly, signed treaties of neutrality to stay out of any potential conflict.

Within a year from the publication of the manifesto, in 1939, the Second

World War was declared. The inhabitants of Rhodes were required to present themselves for individual photographs. Identity work permits and documents classifying their race were issued, food was rationed. The Italians did not enforce the wearing of the yellow badges with the Star of David on their Jewish inhabitants clothing for identification. This was in contrast to the Germans, who made the emblem a mandatory imposition in their spheres of control in Europe.

On occasion, a few of the young men of La Juderia, with the help of their Turkish and Greek friends, decided to leave the island. Waiting for the right timing to go unnoticed, they boarded small fishing craft. Setting off in the pre-dawn hours, they made a twenty-two mile crossing out to sea. The crew, carefully avoiding the Italian patrol boats, headed for the sanctuary of Turkey. Landing on beaches near Marmaris, the men slipped off the boats into the water. Taking in a breath of their new found freedom, they walked or hitched rides along the coastline to Izmir and to the assistance of the Jewish community in that city.

The Turks had always assisted the Jewish community, and gave their help once more; their patrols turned a blind eye to the practice. They allowed the undocumented expatriates to remain in Turkey, and in some cases helped them get to Palestine.

The deepwater facilities of the eastern harbor, two hundred yards from the homes in La Juderia were an important port-of-call for the Italian Navy. The port saw a flow of Italian troops using the facilities as a staging and embarkation point for Mediterranean and Aegean combat.

Allegra continued with her cleaning work at the Italian officers' mess. She had earned a position of trust among the officers who for the most part, ignored her presence, while discussing the war's progress. Mussolini in late 1940 launched an attack for the conquest of Greece from Albania. She overheard the officers talk that the Greeks were putting up a stiffer resistance than expected to Il Duce's assault. In addition, contrary to Germany's lightening victories in the rest of Europe, parts of Southern Italy had fallen to the Allies. The main source of news, amongst her isolated community, was broadcasts beamed by the British Broadcasting Corporation, which was listened to on shortwave radios. Allegra developed into an added source of information for her people in the island.

Vittorio has risen in rank to Captain. Over the years, his feelings for Allegra had grown, but he had with some difficulty, kept from expressing his emotions to her. His discreet inquiries about Allegra's personal life had revealed that when not working, she was with her family and helping other members of the community. To his relief, there was no mention of her having a romantic interest.

Allegra had admired Vittorio's strength of character. She had with time, developed a warm respect for him. Nevertheless, that was the extent to which she would allow her feelings to stretch. She frequently reminded herself that he was an active member of the bureaucracy that imposed such hardships on her people. What she and the community of the walled city were unaware of, was that the Captain was quietly ignoring some of the stern regulations that he had been ordered to impose on them.

By 1941, the tide of war began to turn against Italy. Mussolini failed to take Greece, and parts of Southern Italy fell to the Allies. Hitler turned his attention to making up the losses and covering his flank. He attacked Greece, occupying that country in a matter of days. The Germans established a minor presence on Rhodes alongside their Italian allies. Battles ensued for possession of the Aegean islands. British and German forces attacked and each attempted to occupy and control the strategic port of Rhodes.

CHAPTER 3

THE NIGHTMARE OF WAR

The close proximity of the inhabitants of La Juderia to the deepwater port turned their lives into a survival nightmare. Shells and bombs fell within their immediate area damaging buildings and property. During the hostilities, Isaac, Djoya and Allegra huddled inside their unprotected, small home as earsplitting explosions echoed all the way through the walls around them.

During brief lulls in the fighting, Allegra would take the risk of venturing out into the nearby narrow streets in the hope of finding food to sustain her parents and herself.

While on those short sojourns, Allegra became aware and witnessed how life had become very complicated with regard to the different ethnic nationalities on the Island.

With the fall of Southern Italy and the reinstatement of the King and Queen of Italy in that Southern region, many of the Italians on Rhodes had switched alliances to the British forces. A large number of the Greeks were sympathetic and collaborating with the Germans. Faction fighting had developed between the Italians and Greeks. The Turks had managed to stay neutral and away from the battles between the warring factions. La Juderia, because of its strategic position, was taking a substantial toll from the fighting between the British and German forces.

The Allied Joint Planning Staff had seriously considered the possibility of a major assault on the Dodecanese. Rhodes, and nearby Scarpanto, the two strategically placed islands, were their principal objective. Their planning was complicated by the competing ambitions of the Greeks and Turks who were both vying for ultimate possession of the islands. The British, as a result decided to carry out all operations using only British forces, which put them at a strategic disadvantage.

In September 1943, a clandestine mission under the command of a highly decorated British Officer, Captain A.G. Redfern, MBE, went operational.

Captain Alan Redfern was from Southern Rhodesia. His patrol was part of the Long Range Desert Group that had seen action in North Africa and consisted of six men, plus an interpreter. Their orders were to observe and report on all shipping and air movement in the direction of Rhodes, as well as, to persuade an Italian to go undercover in Rhodes and help stiffen Italian resistance on the island against the Germans.

Slipping out of Leros under the cover of darkness in the early hours of a September morning, the patrol made their way out of Portolago Bay in a light boat, known as a "caique". They stealthily navigated to the island of Simi and then to Panarmiti. There, they were welcomed by an elderly abbot who ran the monastery on the island. The abbot placed his monastery and his men at the disposal of the British patrol. Greek partisans and sympathetic Italian soldiers also offered their assistance to the British soldiers.

The patrol set off by foot on a four-hour climb up a steep cliff that overlooked the sea to the distant island of Rhodes. At the top, Captain Redfern set up the patrol's observation location. From their high vantage position, they were able to watch the activities taking place across the stretch of water on Rhodes. They began observations and intelligence gathering for the next stage of their objective - to cross the stretch of sea to Rhodes and to carry out their clandestine mission against the Germans.

They observed the movement and the attacks by British fighter planes as those aircraft participated in twelve air raids on Rhodes that day.

From his vantage point overlooking Rhodes, Captain Redfern watched the bombs explode on the island and over the deepwater port. He was unaware of an incredible twist of fate that existed between his family and the Hanan family living on Rhodes, nearby that deepwater port. Back home, in the British colony of Southern Rhodesia, Captain Redfern had a wife, a son John, aged five, and a daughter Margaret, aged nine, living in Salisbury. Isaac and Djoya Hanan, also, had family in Southern Rhodesia. They too, lived in the same city. To take the coincidence even further, the captain's daughter, Margaret Redfern and the Hanan's nine-year-old granddaughter, Louise Benatar, were best friends.

On the dawn of the third day, Captain Redfern's patrol watched a refugee rowing boat containing Italian officers arrive on their island. It contained a party of Italian officers led by a colonel who had escaped from Rhodes. A rendezvous was arranged between the British and Italians. The sympathetic Italian officers provided Captain Redfern with a great deal of interesting information and intelligence for their intended clandestine mission to Rhodes.

Captain Redfern completed formulating his plans to proceed to Rhodes. He contacted the Special Boat Squadron arranging transportation to and subsequent evacuation from Rhodes. He was also able to establish a radio communication link with the new supportive Italian commander of Rhodes, Commander Corriadini. The two officers worked on the detailed arrangements for the mission. While the patrol waited for final instructions from Allied Operations, they continued with their observations. Rhodes was being subjected to between eight to twelve Allied air raids and bombing daily.

The Germans for their part maintained a strong air force capability from their bases in Greece and their occupied Aegean islands. They used this advantage effectively, to maintain a constant bombardment of the British forces. The British were able to sustain a small force of fighter aircraft based on the nearby island of Cos. The island was a small one with a single airfield containing multiple landing strips; it did not have the capacity to maintain a large force. It was subjected to lengthy and sustained attacks on its landing strips by the German fighter aircraft. The ever-growing intensity of German air attacks was also preventing the allied shipping from supplying heavy equipment by sea, to support the capture of Rhodes by the Allies. What did make it through the intense aerial assault, had to be shipped in during the darkness of night.

Captain Redfern was advised by operational reconnaissance, that a considerable sized enemy naval convoy was at sea and nearby, heading in his direction. The convoy was assumed to be carrying reinforcements for the German occupation of Rhodes. The German air superiority made it impossible for the Royal Navy to intercept the convoy by day. The Allies now had to rely on mostly nighttime raids, which had minimal effect on slowing the progress of that fleet.

Captain Redfern received the green light for their mission to Rhodes. An advance party consisting of an officer and three of his men, set off under the cover of darkness in a small craft and a dinghy for Rhodes. Captain Redfern received an order from Allied Operations, to remain behind and to wait for an update of his instructions.

At this time, the Germans commenced to intensify their all-out assault attacks - they were positioned to overrun the British held islands. As a result, Captain Redfern received new instructions for an evacuation of his position on Panarmiti and ordered to regroup to the island of Simi. The advance party that had set off for Rhodes was recalled before they could complete their mission. That group was able to return with only two of the men and minus the dingy.

As instructed the patrol made its way down the cliff, returned to the monastery and evacuated by small craft to Simi. On their arrival at Simi, they found that there were no Allied flags left flying; the town had been destroyed, by German air raids and was in flames.

A German occupation of the Aegean Islands was imminent.

Captain Redfern's party sought cover among the hills outside the town of Simi, but they were discovered by overflying enemy aircraft. The patrol came under intense fire from three German Ju 87 Stuka planes, which began a relentless series of dive bomb attacks on the patrol. The attack by those bombers cost the lives of two of the patrol's party.

Captain Redfern and his surviving men subsequently remained and continued to assist partisans in their efforts against the German occupation of the Aegean Islands. Those efforts often times were at great risk and frequently under heavy fire. Captain Redfern was subsequently killed in action on the island of Leros.

The British forces were not equipped with sufficient reinforcements to back up a sustained attack or to accomplish an occupation of Rhodes. Repelling the Allied advances, the Germans occupied the Island of Rhodes in September 1943. The Italian contingent that remained behind on the island was stripped of any authority. Although initially the Italian officers were not incarcerated, they were now treated as adversaries by the German occupying forces.

The new German commanders brutally imposed and established their authority on the population of Rhodes. Food rations were immediately cut in half. Photographs of every single inhabitant were taken and posted on walls. Special identity cards were issued identifying the Jewish population of La Juderia.

Army tanks with their turrets threateningly positioned were temporarily maneuvered to all the entrances and exits of La Juderia as sentries at the Jewish quarter. Its inhabitants became prisoners within the ghetto for several days while the tanks remained menacingly at those posts.

Allegra, with the ousting of the Italian authority, no longer had any work to earn her much needed income. She frequently walked aimlessly along the narrow road near her home taking in the austere measures. She looked around at the stark expressions of fear on her peoples' faces as they sat by the tarnished steps outside their homes. Those who ventured out and walked in the streets of La Juderia did so huddled and spoke in whispers, fearful of being noticed by the new Nazi invaders and terrified of the German reaction.

Allegra, somehow though, sensed that through all this adversity, there was an implicit and bonding power of spiritual belief. The immense feeling of traditional kinship and faith remained a strong affinity factor within her people. She knew it was something that their new Nazi captors were incapable of understanding.

CHAPTER 4

THE GERMAN OCCUPATION

Initially, the military commanders of the German occupying forces were "good" to the inhabitants of Rhodes, including keeping an arm's length distance from the affairs of La Juderia. There were a couple of instances of impropriety carried out by German soldiers, where they would pick on a household and order the members of that family to bring out their possessions. The pretext used was a search for smuggled food and goods. Any reluctance to follow that order was swiftly and fiercely met with beatings upon the terrified family members. Once the possessions were laid outside the home, their valuables and belongings were confiscated. However, it was recognized that in those instances the German perpetrators were punished by their superiors for their improper actions.

There was a veiled designed purpose by the German commanders in their policy of equitable conduct towards the general public. It was a strategy to gain the trust and compliance by the members of the community. They succeeded in fooling the population,

Relations with the Turkish Muslims and Jews on the island had been, and continued to be, excellent. They maintained their lines of communication and their leaders often met to discuss matters of mutual concern. The people in La Juderia and their neighbors in the Turkish quarter often helped each other when the need arose.

The British forces launched attacks of fighter and bomber command aircraft from their bases in Cypress and Malta on the Island of Rhodes. Their targets were three airfields located some distance away from the city, and the prime naval prize of the deepwater eastern port located less than two hundred yards from La Juderia. The attacks occurred mainly on cloudless nights and during moonlit clear weather. The bombing incursions were also launched dependant on the number of German naval ships anchored at the port.

In the course of the raids on the port, many of the bombs missed their mark and struck La Juderia, killing several people and destroying buildings in the Jewish Quarter. With little warning of the deadly incoming bombs, Allegra, Isaac and Djoya with other inhabitants, when not in their homes, had to run for cover and seek shelter from the deadly onslaught, hiding for protection inside the most fortified parts of the old castle fortress in the central square.

During one of those nightly bombing attacks, the great synagogue of Rhodes the "Kehila Grande" and a nearby historic Church were struck by bombs and although still left standing, were badly damaged.

It was harrowing for the people, dashing for shelter as aircraft made their low flying bomb drop approach. The ensuing screeching whistle of incoming missiles, followed by the blasts and flying debris, left emotional scars.

During one such incursion, Allegra and her parents joined the other members of her community to huddle inside a building for shelter. They felt the earth shake around them from several fiery explosions; a friend crouched next to Allegra, lowered her face into her trembling hands and broke down in tears.

"Isn't it enough what we have already endured. Now, our friends are bombing and accidentally killing us, too?" She cried.

Allegra reached over and put her arms around the frightened woman to try to console her. There wasn't anything else she could do to make the situation easier.

During the following weeks, several houses were hit with an additional loss in life. The original old synagogue in Dossiadou Street, the Kahal Shalom and the three other temples, amazingly, remained untouched, despite several properties nearby taking direct hits from bombs.

With the threat of additional bombings and the German occupation, a concern of the Jewish community was the safety of the Sefer Torahs.

The heart and soul of any Jewish community is the Torah. It contains the Old Testament – the five books of Moses. The Rhodes community had preserved several Torahs in their synagogues, including an eight hundred year old Torah brought by their ancestors from Spain. It was one of the oldest in the world.

The elders of the community made a decision to secret the Torahs. The problem they faced was in finding a safe place to hide them for the duration of the war. The leaders of the Jewish community arranged for a private meeting with the Turkish Muslim religious leader, the Grand Mufti of Rhodes, Seyh Suleyman Kaslioglu. During the meeting the Chief Rabbi explained to the

Grand Mufti, the concerns he and his community had over the safety of the Torahs.

The Grand Mufti during the meeting offered to take the Torah scrolls into his possession and hide them for safekeeping. The Chief Rabbi thanked him, but voiced a doubt whether that measure would keep the scrolls safe. The Grand Mufti smiled and answered the Rabbi's concern with a question of his own that resolved the issue.

He asked; "If the Rabbi were a Nazi, looking for a Jewish Torah, would he ever think of looking for it in a Muslim Mosque?"

In secret, the precious Torahs were given to the Grand Mufti for safekeeping. He hid them inside the pulpit of the Morad Reis Mosque. The Mosque, located in the New City outside the old walled city of Rhodes was a safe distance away from La Juderia and the bombings.

It was now early spring 1944. Allegra and her young friends spent much of their time doing community work, helping the older, frail, infirmed and sick members who could no longer cope on their own.

A major portion of Southern Italy had fallen to the Allied forces. Mussolini had temporarily been deposed from power. The King and Queen of Italy signed an Armistice with the Allied forces the previous September, which brought much of the Italian army over to the side of the Allies.

Captain Vittorio and his men were now considered enemy militia by the Germans. As the new occupying forces took control, Vittorio observed the harsh treatment and subsequent internment the German army was meting out to their former Italian allies. He and a small band of his men decided to escape and sought refuge in the mountainous hills outside Rhodes. From this high vantage point captain Vittorio and his men were able to observe the German activities and movements on the island. Routinely, German military scouts searched to expose where Vittorio's now rag-tag group of men were concealed and kept them constantly on the move to avoid capture. Sporadically, firefight clashes ensued as a result of brief contacts between the two militia groups, during the course of which, the Italians became adept at eventually slipping away into the forestry to find another set of hills to hide.

Allegra rarely saw Vittorio, but when the occasional opportunity did arise, he would secret himself into La Juderia. He would bring with him a few stolen vegetables and medical supplies. Allegra passed the supplies on to those needing it the most. It was now clear where Vittorio's affections lay, but Allegra felt guarded to give in to a romantic involvement with him. She did care for him, but restrained her feelings, in the belief that there was too much uncertainty surrounding their lives.

One day, while doing her daily rounds, Allegra came across two children, a boy and a girl. Almost everyone knew each other in the community and she recognized them as members of a local family. The boy was named Samy and twelve years old. The girl was Lucie and ten years old. Samy had his arm over Lucie's shoulders trying to comfort her as she wept. Allegra was aware that their mother had been sick and due to not being able to obtain the proper medication, had recently passed away.

Allegra sat down beside them, "Is there anything I can do to help you?" She asked.

Samy shook his head in response; his large brown eyes sadly looked up at Allegra.

"My sister is crying because she misses our mother."

From then on, Allegra would take the time during her daily rounds to stop and talk with them. She would try to introduce lively chatter during the conversations in an attempt to keep their spirits high. The children often spoke fondly of their father, who was the only parent they had left to look after them. A great friendship developed between Allegra and the two young siblings during those daily encounters.

All through the hardships, the people of La Juderia kept their faith. Each of the holy festivals was observed according to the traditions, many times hidden from the attention of the Germans.

In early March 1944, Isaac, Djoya and Allegra were in their home during the early evening, preparing for the festival of Purim. It was raining outside with heavy overcast clouds. Isaac noted this, and mentioned with a sense of relief that the weather made it unlikely that a bombing raid would take place that night. Sitting down around a rationed candle, Isaac began to say prayers, but, was interrupted by a rapping at the door.

At the door, Isaac saw a man wearing a red fez standing in the rain. The man asked if he could come in. Opening the door the man entered and wiped the rain off his fez. He introduced himself as a messenger from the Turkish Consulate in Rhodes. Reaching inside his jacket, he produced a letter. The envelope was addressed to "Signor Isaac Hanan". The messenger explained that it had been given to the consular office in Southern Rhodesia during late October; 1943. However, the delivery of the letter had taken a long time because of its passage through diplomatic pouches. It had taken several months to arrive at the consular office in Rhodes.

With Djoya and Allegra eagerly looking over his shoulder, Isaac opened the envelope. It was from their children, with notes from Rachel and Raphael and their families in Africa. It also, contained a wad of cash comprised of Italian lira and Greek drachmas.

Included in the news, Rachel in her note told them that she had given birth to her third child, a son on October 10th, 1943. They had in honor of the 'Signor' decided to name the child Isaac, after him.

The dim candle lit room suddenly appeared to brighten.

When the messenger left, Isaac resumed his prayers with Djoya and Allegra. He included additional words in his prayers with a supplication that by the time all his grandchildren reached maturity, the world would be a better place for them to live in. As they sat down to eat a sparse meal, Isaac said with a gentle gleam in his eyes;

"Perhaps when my new grandson, Isaac, becomes a man, he will learn what we endured, know of our experiences, and tell the world."

With winter nearly over, in April, came the first night of Passover –"Erev Pesach," the commemoration of Moses and the departure of Jews from Egypt. The tradition had been for the woman of La Juderia to bake their own unleavened sheaths of bread – "matzos" for the dinner table and the men to attend services at the synagogue.

Djoya and Allegra only had enough dough to prepare for one slice of matzo, but grateful it was adequate for them to fulfill their custom.

As the sun set, it was a clear moonlit night. Isaac, set off to attend the traditional services with the other men at the nearby Kahal Shalom synagogue.

The service commenced, Isaac and the men listened as the beautiful sound of the Cantor's singing filled the synagogue. Isaac's thoughts became lost in contemplation as he became focused on the prayers for this special occasion of Jewish tradition,

Without warning, a loud explosion resonated from nearby. The chandeliers of the synagogue swayed, and the seats shuddered from the impact. Air raid sirens began to wail and the men made for whatever cover they could find within the building.

At their home Djoya and Allegra also felt the nearby explosive impact followed by the wail of loud sirens. Dropping everything, they fled outside their house and ran towards the more fortified buildings for shelter at the center square. Bombs fell around them as they ran, hitting houses, exploding, ripping them apart in blazing balls of fire. The strike this night seemed to be on an intensified level from the prior blitzes from fighter aircraft bombers.

Breathlessly, Djoya and Allegra reached the entrance of the shelter and dashed inside the building. The structure they had chosen for shelter was packed with many people and they edged inside and seated themselves near the entrance.

The bombs exploded all around La Juderia with particular ferocity. Parts of the walls of the shelter splintered and fell to the ground from the force of the surrounding impacts. The ear shattering resonance became louder as the bombs got closer.

A bomb made a direct hit on the shelter.

Voices screamed as walls crumbled, fiery fragments splattered throughout the building's structure.

After what seemed to be an eternity, the bombs finally stopped falling. A few moments of eerie silence followed. People began to emerge from their positions of shelter.

Isaac left the synagogue to see what damage had occurred to and assist any victims. A friend came running past him carrying a bucket of water. Isaac stopped him briefly to ask what had happened. The man informed him that a building used for shelter at the central square had taken a direct hit. Many people had been killed there, and several injured. Isaac inquired who had lost their lives. The friend replied that he did not know who the dead were. The man proceeded running with his water-filled bucket towards the shelter.

As Isaac approached the location used as a shelter, fires were still blazing around the entrance. Against a macabre backdrop of the flames, he could see the shadowy outlines of men fighting the fires. Some were risking injury carrying corpses away from the burning inferno. He increased pace, to assist. Upon seeing Isaac's approach, some of the men in the vicinity stopped what they were doing and grabbed hold of him, pulling him away from the scene. Isaac did not understand what was happening.

He was ushered to a nearby home and sat down inside the living room.

He asked why he had been taken there. The men present turned away their faces and did not answer. After a few moments, the chief Rabbi arrived at the home and sat down next to Isaac. An ominous feeling of fear swept through him.

The Rabbi somberly, informed Isaac, that Djoya and Allegra were amongst those killed by the bomb at the air raid shelter.

The news struck Isaac like a thunderbolt that shattered his life. He was barely able to stand from the shock. A couple of his male friends escorted Isaac to his home and spent that night with him, so that he would not be alone.

The following day a funeral for Djoya, Allegra and eleven additional victims was swiftly arranged. Tradition held that only men attended to the burial, while women and girls stayed home. The entire community of men attended the services at the Jewish cemetery. Isaac said the Kaddish, the prayer of the departed, as he stood by his wife and daughter's gravesides Little Samy had come with his father to pay their respects to Allegra, the woman who had befriended them. He left a small flower on the pile of earth where she was buried.

Outside the cemetery and a distance away from the view of the mourners, another man had come to pay his respects. Captain Vittorio stood discreetly behind the concealment of a wall, heartbroken, and watched the events.

For Isaac, the days after became very difficult. Whenever he returned home, whatever he looked at had memories, the empty chairs, the photos on the walls, the stove still had the fine aroma of food. His eyes would cloud up with the reminders of his wife Djoya and daughter Allegra

But then, those memories were all that Isaac now had left for companionship in his small home.

CHAPTER 5

THE DEPORTATION FROM RHODES ISLAND

Word, somehow, reached Gestapo headquarters in Berlin that a Jewish community of five thousand was "flourishing" on the Island of Rhodes. There was outrage amongst the Nazi High Command that such a situation was allowed to exist. The Gestapo SS - Special Action Einsatz Group and SD - Sicherheitsdienst Security Service were ordered to travel to Rhodes to "resolve the Jewish problem."

The Nazis had miscalculated the number of Jews on the island. Owing to the emigration of many of the younger generation in the earlier years, as well as, subsequent deaths, the population was less. The more accurate figure was now closer to only two thousand inhabitants in La Juderia.

The Gestapo units set up their headquarters in the Luftwaffe Air Force Command center in the new section of the city. The SS and SD troops were well organized and skillfully practiced in their tactics. They were particularly adept in the strategy of the use of deceit and treachery towards their targeted victims.

At first, the SS continued with the militia's policy to be "good" in their treatment, with no hurried oppression of the Jewish inhabitants of La Juderia. The designed purpose of this conduct was to gain the trust and compliance by the members of the community. They continued to succeed with that deception.

The Italians were taking heavy losses in the North of Europe and were now effectively out of the war with much of Southern Italy falling under Allied control. Captain Vittorio and the remaining Italian soldiers seeking refuge amongst the mountainous hills of Rhodes continued to be hunted and targeted as an enemy force by the Nazis.

Skirmishes frequently broke out during contacts between the two former allies.

In the summer of 1944, Captain Vittorio and several of his men were captured and detained as prisoners of war. They were disarmed, arrested and briefly held under armed guard at a German army depot. The SS, under the guise of transporting the Italians to a prisoner of war location, loaded them onto trucks and drove to the hills overlooking the beach village of Faliraki.

In the hills, firing squads had been prepared and were lying in wait for them as the Italian soldiers were offloaded from the vehicles.

Captain Vittorio and his men were made to line up in front of the firing squads and mercilessly executed. They were buried beneath unmarked graves under the ground where they had fallen.

A few days later, on the evening of the 17th, during the searing mid-summer heat of July, Gestapo units began using blow horns to broadcast an order to the inhabitants of La Juderia.

The order announced over and over; targeted all Jewish males aged fourteen to sixty. The men were to present themselves the following day, July 18th 1944, at the Air Force Command Center in the new section of the city. They were to appear with their identity cards and work permits. The announcements informed the community that the men were needed to go to the fields to plant crops. A warning was blared out that there would be reprisals to the entire community for any one person who did not comply with the order.

Not wishing to endanger the lives of their fellow members, all the males presented themselves as ordered the next day. They were rounded up, immediately imprisoned and held under guard within the military barracks.

That evening the women and children waited for their fathers, husbands and brothers to return. As darkness settled, no one returned.

Anxiety amongst those who had remained behind was rife for those men and boys who had not returned. Isaac, in his late sixties, joined the other older men who had been exempt because of their age, helping and calming the terrified women and children.

Little Samy, now thirteen and Lucie now eleven years old stood by the doorway of their home anxiously looking and concerned for the welfare of their father. They spent a sleepless night waiting for him to come home.

The next morning the Nazis were out once more on the streets with their blow horns, blaring out instructions. This time, all remaining inhabitants were to present themselves at the Nazi headquarters. The people were told they would be joining the men taken the previous day and relocated to another place. They were ordered to leave behind all possessions except for food, money and jewelry. The instructions were to bring as much food as they could because none would be provided.

Carrying knapsacks of food and much of their life savings, the frightened elderly, women and children, like sheep, did as they were commanded. They were all grouped together and marched to a secure military air base, some distance from the city.

There, they found their men had been incarcerated at the air force command center, imprisoned inside the buildings and under heavy armed guard. They were instructed to join the men.

An atmosphere of fear encased the two thousand people who now found themselves prisoners. Isaac and the others had no idea why they had been brought to the military air base, or what the SS troops intended to do to them. There was some mention that they were being transferred to a different island.

The men taken the previous day had not been given any food. The new arrivals shared what little provisions they had brought with them.

Samy and Lucie frantically searched for their father. He, too, searched amongst the new arrivals for them. When they found each other, Samy and Lucie fearfully and desperately clung to their father. They did not want to risk losing sight of him again.

The Turkish Consul-General of Rhodes, Selahattin Ulkumen, had watched the Nazi actions from his neutral offices in the new city. His security personnel also kept him abreast of the situation. From their intelligence, he knew the events were a prelude to the deportation of the Jews to concentration camps. He went to the assembly point outside the Nazi headquarters where the inhabitants of La Juderia had been instructed to wait. He warned the women and children lined up in front of the Nazi military not to go into the Nazi building. The Nazi guards present, immediately grabbed hold of the Consul–General and forcibly marched him away.

Ulkumen, a young man in his thirties, with his staff, commenced to work furtively and tirelessly to obtain the release of the Jews detained. They searched through all available documents to establish whether any of the Jewish people had a possible link to Turkish nationality. He was able to come up with a list of forty-two people amongst the detainees.

The brave young Consul-General armed with the documents proceeded to the office of the Nazi commanders. He informed them that the people on the list were Turkish nationals and under Turkish protection. He demanded their release from detention.

His initial demand was turned down.

The German Commander, Von Kleeman, informed the consul that under Nazi law,

"All Jews are Jews and have to go to the concentration camps."

Ulkumen persisted, citing various treaties and neutrality agreements between Turkey and Germany.

He stated that, "Under Turkish law, all citizens were equal. There is no differentiation between citizens who were Jewish, Christian or Muslim".

The Nazi commander, nonetheless, continued to deny a release of the detainees.

Determined to obtain their release, Ulkumen, in a calculated ploy used an effective trump card. He warned the German Commander that this could cause an international incident, and that Turkish neutrality was on the line if his nationals were not immediately released.

With Turkey in such close proximity and its shores clearly visible from the Nazi Commander's Rhodes office, it was a neutrality he was not prepared to risk. The Commander reluctantly ordered the release of the forty-two Jewish individuals.

All the people on the Consul-General's list were located at the detention center and under strict guard returned to the new city. They were ordered to present themselves daily, rain or shine, before eight in the morning for a roll call and interrogation. Specifically targeted and watched by the SS, they were thereafter subjected to harassment by the Gestapo, who often detained them for long periods of time. They were kept in a constant state of fear of being rounded up, detained and deported.

The young Consul-General, Ulkumen, subsequently paid a high price for his bravery in saving the forty-two people. Two weeks later, in retaliation for his assistance to Jews of Rhodes the German Commander Von Kleeman, ordered two Luftwaffe fighter aircraft to strafe and bomb the Turkish consulate. The bombs destroyed the consulate, severely wounding the Consul-General's pregnant wife and killing two of the staff members. The Consul-General's wife, Mihrinissa Hanim, was able to give birth to the couple's son, before dying from her injuries.

The German commanders subsequently disputed any responsibility for the attack. They alleged that British fighter aircraft had carried out the bombing of the Turkish Consulate. A few weeks later when Turkey joined the war on the side of the Allies, the Nazis immediately imprisoned Ulkumen.

The two thousand detainees at the air force barracks were kept in confinement for three days at the air force command center. They had use of running water and toilets, but no food was supplied. They had to make do with the little food they had been able to bring with them.

The real face of the Nazi captors began to unmask itself. On the second day, a German SS Major, accompanied by an interpreter began to dispossess the Jewish prisoners of all their jewelry and lifelong savings. The community members were individually forced to place their valuables inside sacks carried by the SS officer. There was the occasional mild or timid protest, which was ignored, while the Major continued to loot the people. However, even the mild protests ceased after a young teenage girl objected to the removal of a gold chain she was wearing containing the Star of David. The SS Officer ripped the chain from her neck, struck her a hard blow that felled her to the ground and proceeded to kick her, as she lay prone.

On the 21st July, the SS commander of the island sounded the air raid sirens and ordered that all the inhabitants of Rhodes stay indoors. At the same time, the Jewish prisoners were commanded to leave the military field and march to the deepwater port near La Juderia. Cripples and crying children who were unable to keep up were pitilessly struck with whips. At the docks, under the supervision of armed guards and SS attack dogs, the community was loaded into the holds of three old and rusted freighters. The ships they were placed into were severely overcrowded with over six hundred people crammed into each cargo hold. The holds were oppressive from the summer heat, filthy, without water and waste facilities.

Isaac stood in the cramped space of one of the holds, toe to toe with his people. He, like the others now knew they were being taken to Athens. He was unaware of why they were being taken there, or what the Nazis had in store for them.

Isaac did know that he and the others were living out a nightmare. A nightmare from which there was no reprieve of awakening and of escaping the horror.

The freighters remained berthed at the deepwater pier with their human cargoes until the afternoon of July 23rd, when they pulled their moorings and slowly heaved out of the harbor.

CHAPTER 6

THE CRUEL JOURNEY

The Jewish prisoners saw the city of Rhodes move away from them as the overcrowded ships set off at a slow rate of knots for the port in Athens.

There was no food or water supplied. There were no toilet facilities. The mid-summer temperatures seared to well above 100 degrees Fahrenheit, making the rusted metal that held them captives scorching to the touch

The voyage by sea to the Athens port of Piraeus normally took a day and a half to two days to accomplish by boat. The old and slow freighters took ten days to reach Athens.

Without toilet facilities people had to find corners to relieve themselves. The heat exacerbated the terrible smell. Isaac and his friends did the best they could to help their fellow prisoners. Samy and Lucie huddled next to their father, packed in amongst the humanity, in the middle of one of the holds. They tried desperately to survive. Without water, their food running low, combined with rough seas, many of the exhausted and cramped passengers became ill. The community experienced a death among them the first night out the freighters were at sea.

The next morning the freighters docked at a small deserted island. Two men from the community were allowed off the boat with the body to bury the deceased man.

On the second night, the freighters docked at the island of Cos. Ninety-four captive Jewish inhabitants of the island were brought aboard and pressed in among the overcrowded humanity aboard the ships.

The journey continued on to the Greek island of Leros. There, the captain of the boats, an Austrian national, repulsed by the inhuman treatment on the freighters refused to continue under the existing conditions. He demanded that unless food and water were brought aboard, the boats would not travel any further. Only when bread and water were supplied, did he agree to carry on with the voyage.

The freighters did not make any further stops for the remaining several days until the ships reached Athens. During this portion of the voyage a further five members of the community died.

On the tenth day, the three freighters docked at the port of Piraeus. Trucks were waiting for them at the dock and the imprisoned community were loaded into the vehicles and transported to an open field set aside by the Nazis. The field, situated in Haidari, outside the city of Athens did not contain any water or toilet amenities.

Under heavy armed guard, the prisoners offloaded from the trucks at the outer edge of the field. The Nazis proceeded to assemble the community and ordered them to march into the center of the open space. There, they forced the community to sit in the middle of the field. They stayed in that open field for three days without food or water.

The morning of the fourth day, trucks arrived and they were transported to the railway station. SS troops armed with rifles and attack dogs stood by the platforms watching the tired and hungry people arrive.

Trains with cattle carts were waiting for them. With the threat of the dogs being released, the SS ordered the captives to enter inside the confined spaces of the cattle carts.

Exhausted and weak from hunger, Isaac was barely able to raise himself onto the putrid smelling cattle train. With each car filling to eighty persons and overcrowded capacity, people were ushered to enter the next cart, and the next cart, until they were all full. Samy, Lucie and their father following a short distance behind were put in the in the cart adjoining Isaac's. Inside the dark overcrowded confines was the luxury of a barrel set in a corner for people to relieve themselves.

The trains, filled with their cargos of humanity, pulled out of Athens station for what was a journey into horror. The sluggish procession traveled the railroad tracks for twelve days. For some, it was an eternity and a transport to the end of their lives.

Inside his cattle cart, Isaac with tear-filled eyes watched his life-long friends and neighbors of La Juderia suffer from asphyxiation, desperately trying to get to a small opening in the confined carriage to breathe.

He watched them trying to survive the best they could in the overcrowded space, helpless, hungry and filled with fear.

His tears increased as he watched their anxiety and pain when they could no longer physically cope and death overcame them.

In his carriage, Samy made his way to a small crack in the wooden container where he squinted through the opening. He could see buildings and passing scenery the trains crossed but had no idea of where they were.

The first night, the train stopped in what appeared to be the middle of nowhere. The incarcerated were ordered to get off the cattle carts and bring out any dead that were inside. The dead were laid out alongside the railroad tracks.

The German SS troops and their dogs were well trained. They knew exactly what their task was and they strictly and mercilessly carried out their function.

The Jewish captives were told to stand in front of the cattle carts for a head count. No talking was allowed. Groups were severely beaten and the dogs were unleashed to attack and bite people for the slightest transgression.

Terrified, Isaac and the others did precisely what they were ordered to do.

The prisoners were instructed to go back onto the train and the locomotive slowly pulled away once more.

The second and third days followed the same pattern. The prisoners were offloaded. The dead and dying were brought out of the cattle carts and placed alongside the railroad tracks. The head count and beatings took place. The only exception to the pattern was on the third night. The men were allowed to empty the putrid barrels that were used to relieve themselves. The captives were also given a few scraps of bread and a little water.

At some point the procession of trains crossed from Greece into Albania The only solace Samy had was looking through the crack in the cattle cart and watching the scenery pass by. On the fourth day, Samy saw that the buildings and signposts along the tracks were different. He informed his father. Looking through the crack, at the signposts, he told Samy that he believed they had entered Yugoslavia.

By the fifth day when the trains crossed into Croatia, many of the people in the cattle carts had come down with dysentery. Isaac and the members of the community that were alive had done so purely by the instinct to survive.

The sixth day the trains crossed the border into Hungary. That night when the train made its stop, they were allowed to empty once more the putrid barrels.

By the seventh night, Isaac had become weak and feeble. He was barely able to get off the train to attend the regular head count. He stood beside a longtime friend from Rhodes. Isaac pulled out an envelope from his shirt pocket containing cash that had been sent to him by his children. Turning to his friend, he handed the envelope to him, saying;

"If I do not survive, please, can you find a way to get this money back to my family?"

A Gestapo soldier overheard Isaac's words. The man strode over with his rifle raised.

He screamed out, "I told you no talking!"

With that, the soldier brought the butt of his rifle crashing down on the back of Isaac's head.

With his skull fractured, Isaac slumped and fell to the ground. Samy, who was standing nearby recognized that it was his friend Allegra's father, who had been hurt. He started to move toward the injured man to give assistance, but his father pulled him back, fearful that the same treatment would be inflicted on his son.

The SS soldiers completed their head count and ordered the Jewish captives to return inside the cattle cars. With all of them on board, the German soldiers began to check the dead and dying bodies that had been left lying along the railroad tracks.

A soldier came upon the prone body of Isaac. He was barely breathing, from the blood and injuries to his head; he was clearly close to death. The soldier left him lying there and proceeded to pull down the outside bolts of the cattle cars securing the prisoners inside.

The train slowly pulled away leaving the dead and dying together on the side of the rail tracks.

Barely conscious and drawing his last breathes; Isaac heard the sound of the railroad engines as they moved away in the distance and into the darkness of the night. Then, there was a complete silence.

He began to say the Kaddish, the prayer for the dying and dead, for him and those left behind. He looked up at the stars in the clear sky and for the first time in a while, he smiled. He felt a sensation of peace as memories of his wife Djoya, all his children, and Rhodes, flashed through his mind.

Then, he closed his eyes for the last time.

CHAPTER 7

THE ARRIVAL AT AUSCHWITZ

Standing by the crack in his cattle cart fatigued, thirsty and hungry, Samy tried to keep his sanity by watching the passing scenery. None of the people from La Juderia in his cart had ever traveled this far before. Taking turns to look out the crack they could only guess where they were. On the eighth day, some speculated that the trains were now moving into Czechoslovakia.

Lucie had become ill from malnutrition. The only cure for her was food and medication, and they had none. Her father cradled her lovingly in his arms; it was all he could do to try to alleviate her suffering. He wondered how much longer they would have to endure inside the locked confines of the cattle carts in this unrelenting journey, and what purgatory awaited them at their destination.

Close to Samy, an elderly woman gasped for air and slipped into unconsciousness. The packed and severely overcrowded space within the cattle cart afforded little room for maneuver. Those in the confined space around her shuffled and shifted to help move her limp body close to the small air crack at the wall of the cattle cart to give her a turn at some relief to breathe.

The ninth and tenth days continued with the same brutality at the hands of the guards at the nighttime stops and the captives' ongoing struggle for survival.

On the eleventh day, Samy noticed through the crack in the cart, that there was something very different in the passing scenery, with the appearance of large factory-like structures and abandoned villages. Several of the people in the cart looked through the wooden fracture unable to identify their surroundings. One individual ventured that they may have entered Poland.

On the twelfth day, while it was very early morning and still in the darkness of night, the train slowed down and maintained its travel at a lower rate of speed. Samy peered out through the crack. In the distance, he could see lights encircling a conglomeration of brick buildings surrounded by tall wire fences. In the middle of the structures, he saw a large brick stack billowing out black clouds of smoke. The train proceeded into a rail yard separating the buildings. The buildings were bordered on each side of the rail tracks with tall-electrified barriers. On one side of the fences he could see a few gaunt men wearing dirty, thick pin striped pajama-like clothing, on the other side there were thin, paled, head shaven, women.

They had entered the Auschwitz-Birkenau concentration camp. The survivors of the arduous journey from the community of La Juderia had arrived at their destination.

The cattle carts were swung open and they were all ordered to get off the trains. Outside the trains, SS troops with rifles and attack dogs were waiting. The dogs were released and the troopers commenced to beat the offloading arrivals. Behind the SS came the "Kapos" - prisoners who had been recruited by the SS to do their dirty work. The Kapos separated the people into two groups, one of woman and the other of men. Lucie was pulled forcibly away from her tight grip of her father and brother Samy to be placed with the women.

The eighteen hundred men, women and children were ordered to strip off all their clothing for inspections. Naked and humiliated, they stood and watched as their clothing was inspected for bugs and lice. Soldiers looked them over for any visible illness and scabies. Powerful hoses were then turned on them for a cleansing.

They stood for hours waiting to be processed. Eventually, being ushered into a hall they were formed into two lines, women and children on one side, the men on the other. At the very front, seated at desk, was a uniformed German doctor flanked by SS guards.

The doctor had the incredible power of life and death by the slight movement of his forefinger to the left or to the right. From a mere cursory glance of the individual moved from the line to the front, he would gesture left, which meant death and the gas chamber. A movement of the finger to the right meant temporary life and the slave labor camp.

From their positions in line, Samy and his father fearfully watched the doctor. They saw him casually determine who would live and who would die. To children, their mothers, the aged and those too weak to work, his finger gestured to the left and the gas chambers.

Many of La Juderia saw their fathers, mothers, children, and siblings for the last time.

The Kapos, who were mostly German criminals who had been sentenced to Auschwitz, led the prisoners away to the showers. The "showers" were disguised rooms, which were really gas chambers. Without some of the prisoners fully succumbing to death, their bodies were lifted and thrown into the adjoining furnaces of the crematorium to be burnt and disposed.

There were very few exceptions to the women; most of whom were sent to the gas chambers. It was with overwhelming relief Samy and his father saw somehow, the gesture to the right for Lucie, when she reached the top of the line.

Samy's father reached the front and the slight gesture of the finger was to the right and to life for him. Samy did not watch which way the doctor pointed for his destiny, he unknowingly, followed his father to the right.

Close to one thousand five hundred members of La Juderia were gassed to death that day and their bodies burnt in the crematoria. Their remains became a part of the thick black clouds billowing from the tall chimneystack that engulfed the air of Auschwitz-Birkenau.

Those designated to live were led away by the Kapos to have their heads shaved, sprayed for disinfection and showered. Then, they were taken to a place where each had a tattooed number branded into their forearms. Samy, following closely behind his father, received the next consecutive number to his father embedded in his skin. From that moment, any dignity of a name was removed and each prisoner was solely identified by those numerals. The identifying number was recorded and each given a prison uniform. The uniforms were old and dirty and had obviously been worn many times previously. The uniforms looked like pajamas with white and dark stripes of equal width running vertically. They were so worn out that it was impossible to tell whether the dark stripes were originally blue or black. The prisoners were allocated a bare minimum of rations to keep them alive, sufficient only to sustain them for work. It consisted of half a pound of bread and a pint of coffee for breakfast and a liter of turnip and potato soup for lunch. The Kapos, who were entrusted with ladling out the soup, ensured that the thicker more nourishing contents at the bottom were kept for themselves. The other prisoners had to make do with the more watery substance at the top of the pots.

Samy knew that soon he and his father would look like those gaunt men wearing dirty uniforms he had seen when the cattle trains first arrived at Auschwitz.

The Kapos took them to housing barracks termed "Laagers" which were to be their cellblocks. From here, they would have to arise at dawn each day to go to their assigned slave labor work. Inside their block, there was housing for thousands of inmates. Five and sometimes as many as nine people were allocated to one simple hard wooden bunk and a blanket.

Samy and his father were assigned their temporary work duties. His father was immediately to join work groups carrying coal to the factories.

Samy was to join two work groups. Firstly, at dawn, his job was to consist of removing dead bodies from the electrified fences surrounding the camp. With that completed, he was to work for the rest of the day picking crops in the fields.

That night, Samy and his father saw the other male inmates return from their labors. They looked haggard, tired and hungry. Some men were so thin that their bones were clearly protruding from what was left of their emaciated skin. They looked like walking skeletons and living corpses.

Samy had no concept of what the work of removing bodies from the electrified fences entailed. He asked one of the inmates working in that detail, a young boy of thirteen, like him, to explain about the labor. The boy was Sephardic, originally from France and able to converse in the universal Judeo-Spanish language, ladino.

The boy told him that the bodies were of inmates who weak, tired, and ill, had, in desperation to escape from their sufferings, committed suicide. Many of them had already been selected to die in the gas chambers the following day. This was their way of cheating their executioners of the power over their lives. Their final act in this world was to throw themselves against the electrified fences. His and Samy's job was to pry the dead from the fences, place them in wagons or wheelbarrows and transport the remains to the crematorium for disposal.

A shudder ran up Samy's spine as he listened to the boy and of the work, he was detailed to carry out.

Samy and his father found a small space on their overcrowded bunk to rest, there was only enough room to sit upright. They were exhausted and distraught, but finding the escape of sleep that first night became unattainable; they were too apprehensive about Lucie and her fate.

At dawn under the supervision of Kapos, Samy joined his work detail to proceed to the electrified fences. He had lost track of the days, but knew it was the second week of August.

At the fences, Samy was met with sights that he could never have imagined in his worst nightmares. There were several bodies of men, fused to the wire. Their bodies were badly marked with burns and the disfigured expressions of pain from the electrification remained frozen on their faces.

The Kapos checked with the SS guards to ensure that the electricity was turned off and ordered the detail to remove the bodies. The most difficult part for Samy was prying the dead men's hands from their death grip on the fences. When the bodies had been delivered to be burnt at the crematorium, the detail proceeded for the work in the fields.

The day's labor at the concentration camp ranged from twelve to fourteen hours, from early morning until the evenings. The weather was always bitterly cold, particularly in the mornings, and often fell below the freezing level. The lack of proper nourishment and scant pajama–like clothing for protection made the frigid conditions hard to endure. However, working with the winter crops, became a source of relief for Samy, away from the scenes of death that he had earlier encountered.

During a lunch break, Samy, wanting to make a new friend, sat next to the boy he had worked with during the dawn detail. They chatted, and the boy told him his name was Aaron. The subject came up regarding the work at the electrified fences and the suicides. Samy told Aaron that it was sad to see those people who had eluded the gas chambers, succumbing to committing suicide. The boy's lips parted on his skeletal face into what looked like a fatalistic smile. Aaron responded that not being sent to the gas chambers, with the others, upon arrival in Auschwitz was only a temporary reprieve. Aaron went on to explain; most laborers did not survive at the camp for more than two months before ultimately dying or being exterminated. Starvation and illness killed a fair amount of them. Then, there were the periodic weekly inspections by the doctors where laborers had to line up for an inspection to determine whether any were too weak to continue work. Any hint of weakness, illness, or infirmary needs, meant being taken to the gas chambers and executed. The constant daily arrivals of new captives on trains from all over Europe, ensured that there was always a fresh supply of laborers to put to work. So, Aaron explained to Samy, some of those who had thrown themselves against the fences were only hurrying the inevitable. They either were too weak, ill, or just did not care anymore, to continue with the slave labor. Knowing their time was limited to days before being sent to the gas chambers, they had taken control of their fate and taken action to bring their misery to an earlier end.

Samy bowed his head in thought. He determined that he had not gone through all the ordeals of survival, to die in this place.

That night Samy met his father after work, they proceeded to the wire fencing which divided them from the railway line and the women's fence on the other side. They called out to the women passing by on the other side for their help. They described Lucie and asked for a message to be passed by word of mouth, for her to meet them after work at that fence. The women, to whom they spoke, promised to do what they could to help.

The second night Samy and his father did the same at the fence and again asked the women to assist passing the message.

The third night, Lucie appeared and waited for them on her side of the fence. Tears streamed down Samy and his father's faces as they saw her. Her head had been shaven and her arm tattooed. However, to their relief, she was alive!

CHAPTER 8

THE HORROR OF AUSCHWITZ

Lucie told her father and Samy that she had been put to work laboring with the women in the section known as "Canada" in Birkenau. She explained; that "Canada" was a cynical term, based on the Polish expression of viewing valuable and fine gifts. She and the women in that sector sorted out the belongings of the prisoners and new arrivals for use by the Germans.

She went on to tell them that she was scared, as there were only a few girls her age in the women's sector. She had noticed during her two days in "Canada" that young girls were selected from the work detail by a doctor and taken away for experimentation. The girls had never returned.

Samy and his father did their best to console the eleven-year-old girl that she would be all right. As they parted, their father cautioned Lucie never to let the Nazis know if she became ill. She was to feign at all times that she was in good health.

Every evening when they had completed their labors, the three met at the fenced barrier. It became their only solace in a living purgatory. Samy and Lucie began to develop a routine of signals that enabled them to communicate better across their divided barricades.

For Samy, despite the dividing barrier between them, that appointment at night with his sister, gave him an added strength and the courage to continue to survive.

Working in the fields Samy began to grasp the immensity of Auschwitz with its numerous compounds of buildings. From the fields, he observed the daily arrivals of trains from all over Europe. From their cattle carts and carriages thousands of people were offloaded. Those who had been allowed to travel with suitcases had them confiscated by the Kapos, their belongings sent for sorting in the Birkenau "Canada" sector. Most of the people would within a few hours of their arrival be taken to be killed in the gas chambers. The billowing black smoke from the crematorium chimneys never stopped rising in thick clouds to hang all pervading over the camps.

Samy learned Auschwitz consisted of three main camps. There was Auschwitz 1 the original and administrative center for the whole multiplex of concentration encampments. It contained a large crematorium, execution yard for firing squads, and a hospital where the head doctor, Joseph Mengela, took twins and dwarfs for sinister experimentation.

The bowels of Auschwitz 1 contained the prison within a prison, where some prisoners who broke the "rules" were forced to spend the night with three others in a box two yards square. They were termed the "standing cells" because there was only room to stand. The basement contained "starvation cells" where prisoners incarcerated in them were given neither food nor water and starved to death. Also, in the basement were the "dark cells", cells with solid doors and a tiny window. The prisoners placed there suffocated to death.

Samy thought about the Nazis who had created such horrific places. He wondered whether they had nothing better to do with their lives other than to dream up such macabre places to kill.

Samy and his father were in Auschwitz 2, the largest of the camps. Its complete name was Auschwitz-Birkenau Concentration and Extermination camp. Most of the new arrivals from France, Germany, Holland, Hungary and the other parts of German occupied Europe passed through these gates. It held hundreds of thousands of inmates and was the killing site of many more than that number. The prisoners were mostly Jews, but there were, also, a large number of Poles and Gypsies.

Auschwitz-Birkenau had four large gas chambers; which were structured and designed to look like showers. The Nazis used a cyanide gas produced from Zyklon B pellets to kill their intended victims. Next to the gas chambers were four crematoria used to incinerate the bodies. As many as twenty-thousand people could be gassed and cremated each day. The death chambers were partly staffed by Sondercommandos, prisoners who worked under the supervision of the SS.

Altogether, six thousand SS troops worked at the camp.

Auschwitz 3 was composed of forty satellite camps surrounding the first two camps. The largest of these camps was Monowitz. They were work camps for German factories populated mostly by Poles forced from their villages into slave labor.

A few of the Kapos selected by the SS to keep order in the barracks were Jewish. Desperate to survive they had accepted the position and collaborated with the Nazis - their fellow members of the Jewish community despised them for accepting this work. However, even the Kapos were not immune from the wrath of the SS guards.

One morning, while Samy was working in the fields, an SS sentry observed a Kapo trying to secrete food inside of his prison garb. The food was freshly picked turnips. The German guards surrounded him; he was marched away to an execution wall and shot.

Samy and his father had to attend periodic inspections, usually once a week and sometimes more often. During these inspections, several hundred men were marched to an open square in the "Laager". There, they were ordered to strip naked for examination, and their clothes checked. Samy noticed several of the men, skeletal from starvation, jogging on the spots where they stood. Samy in a whispered voice asked his new friend Aaron, why they were doing that. Aaron had whispered back that the men were trying to show that they were still fit to work.

Samy felt his nerve endings raw and prickling with fear during the inspections.

Several men did not have their clothes returned; those were the inmates marked for elimination. Naked and emaciated they were marched off by the guards to the gas chambers.

Always grateful for their time together at the separating fence in the evenings, Samy, his father and Lucie continued to meet. Their conversations and signals usually focused on the trivial, such as attempting to throw their meager ration of bread to each other. They avoided talk of the experiences they had each witnessed during the day.

Samy and his father's return to their cellblock in the barracks at night was something that afforded little solace. Disease in the block was rampant. Malnutrition had deprived many of the inmates' bodies from the nutrients to sustain their immune systems. Starving and ill, those who could still walk wandered about aimlessly. Succumbing to starvation and their illnesses, men in their cramped spaces or lying on the floor between bunks, died.

It seemed that to achieve survival for any extended length of time at Auschwitz–Birkenau was an impossible feat to accomplish. At thirteen, Samy found himself faced with a constant flirtation with the outstretched hands of death. He and the other inmates were exposed to dying from hunger, death from the hard work, death from illness or death from exposure to the icy cold weather. Somehow, though, death did not seem ready to reach out to take the thirteen-year-old boy. Samy however, began to experience feelings of guilt. At the time of his arrival at Auschwitz, he had watched his relatives, friends, classmates and young boys ranging in age between fourteen to sixteen years of age, all selected and go to the gas chambers. He felt an immense guilt that he had survived by not watching which direction the doctor's finger had pointed out for his fate. Instead, he had followed his father in his desire to be close to him.

One week later, the same doctor made a second round of selections. Having considered that in the commotion of the original selections for the gas chambers, some intended for extermination may have slipped into the working groups.

This time, Samy was chosen amongst twenty other inmates to be eliminated in the gas chambers. The twenty selectees were immediately removed from the other workers and marched to the front edifice of the gas chambers. The terrified people knew what was in store for them.

At this time, a large contingent of Hungarian Jews had arrived by train into the concentration camp and was being processed into Auschwitz. The gas chambers and crematoria were being utilized to maximum capacity exterminating the mass of new arrivals. Samy and his group had been designated for immediate gassing and disposal, but there was no room to accommodate them.

Samy and the men with him were put on the waiting list. They were to wait to be eliminated and placed on hold two steps away from the entrance to the doors of the gas chambers. They remained there an entire day and night. The men huddled together, terrified and trembling with fear as they waited their turn to look death in the face.

The following morning Samy and his group heard the dreaded command from an officer at the gas chamber entrance, directed at them;

"Raus! Raus! Schnell! Schnell!"

Their turn had arrived!

The doors to the gas chambers opened. Samy could feel his legs trembling with fear as some of the group members looked each other in the eyes in a final gesture of goodbye.

Instead, by some amazing twist of fate, it turned out that the officer barking out the orders was looking for men to assist filling a void with work. A train loaded with potatoes had arrived in the train yard. The potatoes were intended as supplies for the German SS troops. The officer had gone out into the fields to find workers to unload the train, but had found that the workers there had already been moved on to other assignments. Unable to find laborers from the fields the officer had decided to proceed to the gas chambers and find men to unload the train. It was irrelevant whether the men selected to do the work went into the gas chambers this day or merely postponed their execution to the following day: The potatoes needed to be unloaded.

Samy's group and approximately another hundred prisoners were taken off the list to go into the gas chambers. They were given precise orders to proceed immediately to offload the supplies from the train for distribution to the German mess.

As Samy worked hard all day unloading the sacks, he could not help but wonder what had happened, and a thought kept running through his mind;

"A train load of potatoes arrived at Birkenau to remove me from the gas chambers!"

They worked all day and into the evening and through a change of guard in the shift of German soldiers watching the workers. When the unloading of the potatoes was complete, the new shift of guards did not have precise orders of where to return the workers. Through an obvious miscommunication and not having precise orders, they returned them to their original laager with the other regular workers. They had escaped the gas chambers.

As Samy sat amongst the prisoners in his laager, the thought of wonderment kept running through his mind;

"I am alive because a train of potatoes arrived at Birkenau!"

Samy, in due course, discovered that pockets of resistance movements existed among the inmates in the barrack cells. They were unlike the usual style of resistance groups found elsewhere. Owing to the high mortality rate of prisoners, its members generally, never lived long enough to be effective.

The Nazi administration was purposeful in debasing the prisoners to the standard of animals. The resistance groups considered that by maintaining the will to live amongst prisoners was an act of insurgence in itself. It was a goal hard to maintain faced with starvation, deprivation, illness, and humiliation. The inmates were too physically drained and in addition did not have the weaponry to carry out an active physical insurgence.

One of the older surviving resistance groups "Kampf Gruppe Auschwitz" focused instead on individual attempts of escape. It had been formed a year earlier in 1943. The essence being, if successful, the escapee would inform the Allies of the torturous conditions of Auschwitz. The goal was to present a living witness to what was happening at the camp, and bring the possibility of help.

Each escape had to be very carefully planned, because whether successful or not, the wrath of the Nazis would subsequently be imposed with dire consequences on the remaining inmates.

Since the inception of Auschwitz, roughly seven hundred attempts were made to escape. Fewer than three hundred had been successful. If an inmate was caught attempting to escape, the standard punishment, was to be placed in the "starvation cells" of Auschwitz 1 to starve to death.

The regular daily roll calls kept a very tight account of the number of inmates. If the Nazis determined that a successful escape had been made; ten random members of his cellblock would be pulled out and immediately executed. Additionally, if family members of the escapee were still alive, they too would be executed.

Samy considered offering his name on the resistance group list as a potential escapee, but then thought of his father and Lucie - the price was too high!

Samy's new friend, Aaron was the last surviving member of his family. His mother, father and two brothers had been wiped out in the gas chambers on their arrival at the camp. Feeling that he had nothing more to lose, he met with the groups' committee to have his name placed on the list.

A few days later, Samy noticed that Aaron was missing from the dawn work detail due to remove the bodies of the suicides from the electrified fences. Proceeding to the fences, Samy began the usual work with the others to pry bodies from the fences and lift their corpses onto the carts. In the distance, he heard a sudden commotion of dogs barking and SS troops shouting. The disturbance continued for a few more minutes. Guards from the other side of the fences began to run in the direction of the commotion with their rifles at the ready. Then the shouting abruptly stopped, followed by an eerie quiet.

After Samy and his detail completed work at the fences, their SS guards instructed the group to return to the barrack laager, instead of proceeding to their usual labor in the fields.

Positioned in the center of the laager parade square the men saw Aaron. He was standing with a bloodied and drooped head. SS guards stood watch on either side of him.

The SS commander marched to the front of the assembled men. Over a blow horn, he announced that Aaron had attempted to escape and had not made it further than three hundred yards outside the camp. He said that to show that this kind of activity would not be tolerated; ten men from the prisoners' ranks would be selected for execution.

Samy held his breath as the SS guards slowly walked past him and stopped among other inmates, picking out ten men at random. The men chosen were marched in front of Aaron to illustrate to him and the others, what his attempt was going to cost in lives. The SS guards proceeded to take those men selected away from the laager for immediate execution before a firing squad.

As Aaron was led away by the SS guards to Auschwitz 1 and the starvation cells, he turned his head; his sunken eyes looked towards Samy in farewell.

The Nazi administration at Auschwitz kept an accurate record of its activities at the camp. In particular, they had a penchant for taking photographs of the killings and atrocities they carried out. Two inmates, Rudolph Vrba and Alfred Wettzler, managed to get their hands on some of the photographs. With the help of the resistance group, they were able to engineer a successful escape. Risking a trek through German occupied territory, they covertly worked their way to the front lines of the Allied forces.

The escapees discovered that the Allies were barely aware of the existence of Auschwitz. The previous reports by the few inmates, who had escaped and made it to the Allies telling of mass killings, had been dismissed as "exaggerations".

Equipped with the photographs and providing detailed reports, the two escapees were able to convince the Allied leaders of the true circumstances surrounding the activities at Auschwitz.

The British Prime Minister, Winston Churchill, ordered that a plan to bomb Auschwitz or the railway lines leading to it be prepared. However, he was advised that the bombing of the camp would result in a high death toll of prisoners and unlikely to bring to an end the killing procedures. In addition, that bombing of the railway lines was not technically possible.

As result, the hoped for relief by the inmates and resistance group at Auschwitz did not come.

CHAPTER 9

THE STRUGGLE FOR SURVIVAL

The continual increase of deportees arriving by train at Auschwitz saw a swell in the numbers the Nazi SS sent to the gas chambers. By the first week of September, the gas chambers and crematoria exceeded the daily capacity of twenty thousand victims.

The crematoria, as a result, were unable to cope with the number of bodies that needed incineration. Samy and his work detail at the fences were instructed to convey and leave the bodies they collected outside the crematoria for disposal at a later time. As Samy worked to offload the bodies from his wagon, he stopped and paused to look at the horrific sight in front of him. His body froze with the shock of seeing the piles of carcasses waiting for disposal. His stomach had very little inside but that did not stop him from throwing up violently.

The SS guard supervising the detail, walked up, rammed his rifle butt into Samy's side as a chastisement, and instructed him to get back to work. Painfully, Samy picked himself off the ground and continued to offload the corpses.

That night Samy told his father what he had seen and what had happened. His father gently put his arm around his shoulders and said,

"Son, there is much that we are seeing with our eyes that our minds are incapable of digesting. It is important for you to focus on surviving. Survive, so that one day you can tell the world what your eyes have seen."

Samy never forgot those words. He determined to stay alive. The trouble was that he had been watching his father getting thinner; his father's health was deteriorating from starvation.

Despite the number of people killed in the gas chambers, the small percentage that survived swelled up the number of prisoners in the cellblocks.

A fear began to spread among the weaker and senior imprisoned inmates that they soon would be selected for elimination.

During the nights, Samy listened to the accounts of terror the new arrivals in his cellblock had experienced in their home countries. Many of their communities had put up some form of resistance before incarceration and transport to Auschwitz. Some were from Lodz, the last Jewish ghetto to fall in Poland. Sixty thousand people had once lived there before it was liquidated and its inhabitants brought to the camp. A number had been brought from Holland, they told stories of their struggle and how local people and the resistance had tried to help save them. Others were from Hungary. Despite a German agreement that Hungarian Jews would not be deported to concentration camps, the Nazis had reneged on their word. They told of how the Nazis were attempting to wipe out the Jewish populations city by city in Hungary as well.

Among a few of the new arrivals were Poles and Gypsies. The Gypsies were particularly targeted by the Nazis for elimination and were given the worst of the assignments.

Two new children, young boys of thirteen like Samy, had been assigned as replacements to his work detail. Samy saw the reaction of pure horror on their faces as they began their first day of removing bodies from the electrified fences. During the lunch break in the fields, the boys sought out Samy to ask him questions. Samy recalled how only a few weeks earlier he had been the newcomer asking the same from Aaron. In the eternity of a short span of time, he was now the "seasoned" inmate giving similar counsel to that which he had received.

Samy only asked the boys their names and the countries they were from. He did not want to know more about them. His defense mechanism had taken hold, to prevent getting too close to anyone new and the pain it brought with subsequent loss, as he had experienced with Aaron.

During one of their regular evening meeting with Lucie, she related to Samy and her father that the women's sector had also experienced an increase in numbers. She spoke of the fact that there were now a few more young girls closer to her age in her barrack cells. One of the girl's had in particular caught her attention. The girl was among the recent arrivals of families from Amsterdam, Holland. She only knew her as "Anne" and at fifteen, was a few years older than Lucie. Anne had talked with Lucie and the other girls in her barracks about the time prior to her being brought to Auschwitz.

Anne had shared that she and her family had spent two years hiding in their father's office space in Amsterdam. They had successfully evaded capture by the Nazis during that time with the help of their Dutch friends. They were ultimately betrayed by collaborators and captured by the SS. Her family had been imprisoned and taken into solitary confinement at a Dutch prison. They were subsequently taken to Camp Westerbork, a transit camp. From there Jews, Gypsies, and members of the Resistance in the Netherlands were deported to the concentration and extermination camps.

Since her arrival in Auschwitz, Anne had spent her free time collecting scraps of blank paper. At night, she would write on those papers with whatever utensils were available, recording all that she had experienced. The other women in the barracks had encouraged her in the hope that one day someone would read her diary of events and know of the atrocities they had experienced.

Samy and her father were relieved to know that Lucie was now in the company of girls nearer to her age.

The weekly inspections for the men conducted by doctors in the laager as expected, became more harrowing. A greater number of individuals were selected for execution in the gas chambers. Additionally, the lack of disease control in the barracks was resulting in a large number of the inmates becoming ill and infected by typhus. The contamination was widespread amongst the occupants of the barrack cells. Samy's father caught the infection, became very ill with the fever, and lapsed into delirium.

Desperate to help his father, Samy tried to find a way to locate medicines or something else that would help. Nothing was available. He dared not try to get pills from the Nazis, as that would have drawn their attention to his father's condition and with it the certainty of his being taken to the gas chamber.

Samy watched his father wither and eventually pass away.

The longest walk of Samy's young life was going to the meeting place at the dividing fence that evening. He told Lucie that their father had just died. He wanted to reach out to her and cling to her as she broke down and cried. However, the Nazis and the fenced barrier made that feat impossible. Now orphaned, all they had was each other remaining in this unforgiving nightmare.

The dread of the daily work and malnourishment was an unrelenting part of the existence at the concentration camp. At times, Samy thought he would not make it through the day. Nevertheless, he somehow, plucked up the courage to keep going with a determination and will to survive.

While working in the fields a week after his father passed away, Samy heard a loud rumbling noise in the air around him. He paused working to look up at the skies and his eyes encountered the most beautiful sight he had ever seen. The heavens were full of American bomber and fighter aircraft flying overhead.

The Allies had ordered one hundred and twenty-seven B-17 bombers with an escort of one hundred P-51 fighter aircraft to strike the main IG Farben plant that made synthetic oil, as well as the other factories of the adjacent Auschwitz-Monowitz camp.

Samy and the other laborers at Auschwitz-Birkenau stopped their work to watch. They began to cheer as the American aircraft began their bomb dives. Over thirteen hundred bombs, weighing five hundred pounds each, began to cascade out the aircraft bomb doors and fall on the German factories.

It was an amazing sight, as each bomb fell and ripped into the Nazi structures, its impact was accompanied by a feeling of exuberance and hope for the prisoners of Auschwitz. Aware of the possibility that the bombs would bring death to them as well, that worry presented little concern, it was a death they no longer feared.

One of the B-17 pilots accidentally released his bombs intended for the IG Farben plant early; the bombs plummeted down striking one of the civilian barracks in Auschwitz-Birkenau. Several prisoners were killed.

The accidental release of the bombs convinced the inmates below that their camp would be the target of the next strike and that would bring them the salvation they hoped would come. However, apart from that unintentional strike, Auschwitz-Birkenau remained untouched by the bombs.

The prisoners remained confident that this was the first of many strikes. The Allies, they believed, were sending help. The resistance groups began to formulate plans and organize themselves to act when those future strikes occurred. Their plan was to take effect during the ensuing bombardment and chaos that followed. They were going to use that opportunity to revolt against their Nazi captors. The resistance groups discussed the consequences of their rebellion. There was a consensus that their cost in human lives would be very high, but that was something that they accepted and came to terms with. It was a price they were all prepared to pay. This course of action, at least, offered some hope for those that survived.

With their plans in place, the prisoners of Auschwitz waited for the next aerial bombardment by the Allies to take place.

They waited, and waited, the strike and hoped for help never came. Samy, as well as the inmates of the concentration camp began to believe that the Nazi factories were of more importance to the Allies than their lives.

CHAPTER 10

THE UPRISING AND CONSTANT TOIL TO SURVIVE

Each day, Samy would proceed, after his labor at the electrified fence, to the fields with his eyes often searching the skies. While he worked, his ears remained honed for any positive sign of incoming Allied aircraft.

In the evenings, Lucie would often watch Samy as his eyes scanned the skies in optimistic search of the hoped for bomber support as they talked. He shared with his little sister the belief that the Allies would still in spite of everything, one-day come to their help.

Then, one evening in early October, Lucie did not show up at the fence.

Samy waited for her as long he could, it was well into the darkness of night when he slowly walked away. Feeling anxious and worried he went back to his barrack cell. The following evening Samy overwhelmed with a feeling of anxiety returned to their meeting place at the dividing fence.

Again, Lucie did not show up.

Samy called across to the women on the other side of the fence to ask if they had any news of his sister. The women in the proximate area were all new arrivals to the camp; they did not know Lucie and had no information about her to pass on.

Again, Samy waited as long as he could.

Samy went to the fence on the third night. He waited. There was still no sign of Lucie. His heart sank, he guessed what had happened and that she was not going to come back.

In his grieving heart, he knew she was dead.

In the remote hope there would be some sign of Lucie, Samy returned once more to the fence and waited. It was the last time he went to their meeting place. He knew there was no possibility of seeing her again.

With no outside help imminent and the hopes of an aerial strike to spark a revolt diminishing, some of the inmates of Auschwitz-Birkenau took their destiny into their own hands.

The camp resistance learned that the Sondercommandos working at one of the crematoria were due to be murdered on the morning of October 7th, 1944. The resistance passed on this information to that group.

The Sondercommandos were the Jewish slave laborers assigned to work at the crematoria. They were forced into that position by the SS and many accepted such work because it meant a few more days or weeks of life for them. Those who refused the work were immediately executed. The killing in the gas chambers was strictly carried out by the SS guards. The Sondercommandos duties were to dispose of the corpses. Because of their personal knowledge of the clandestine methods the Nazis employed in carrying out exterminations, the Sondercommandos were murdered and replaced at frequent intervals. The Nazis did not want such information to reach the outside world.

The Sondercommandos of Auschwitz-Birkenau 3, with the help of the women inmates assigned to a nearby weapons factory were able to smuggle explosives into their camp.

On the morning of October 7th, 1944, the revolt began.

Using makeshift weapons they utilized stones, axes, hammers, their work tools and homemade grenades, they attacked the SS guards. The SS were taken completely by surprise. Using that element of surprise, the few hundred Sondercommandos overpowered the SS and took control of Crematorium 4. During the course of the fighting, four SS guards were killed and many more were injured. One of them, a German Kapo who had taken cruel amusement by throwing living prisoners into the burning crematorium ovens, was himself thrown into an oven.

Carefully, the Sondercommandos strategically laid out their explosives around the facility. The explosives were detonated resulting in the complete destruction of the crematorium

The Nazi SS guards were not used to having their authority challenged or having to defend themselves. They ran to and from the zone of the hostilities in complete confusion. The entire area transformed into a battlefield.

Samy was working in the fields when he heard an explosion erupt from the site of the crematorium. Looking in that direction he saw the eruption turn into a ball of fire and smoke rising upwards towards the skies. Sirens began to blare; the SS guards supervising his detail went on full alert. Samy and his coworkers were rounded up and made to march back to their prison barracks with the SS guards aiming their rifles menacingly at them.

At this time, the Birkenau Kommando 1 at Crematorium 2 joined the uprising. They also, were able to overpower their guards and broke out of the compound. They did not have explosives, but tore down the surrounding labor camp fences enabling some of their fellow prisoners to escape. During the fighting, that took place two hundred and fifty-two Sondercommandos were shot and killed by the SS.

The revolt and hoped for mass uprisings was crushed and concluded in failure by the end of the day.

All of the prisoners who escaped were captured and rounded up by nightfall. The same day, they, with two hundred Sondercommandos who had not perished during the uprising were forced to strip naked. They were ordered to lie face down on the ground. The SS walked systematically among the rows of prone prisoners shooting each one in the back of the head.

A total of four hundred and fifty-one Sondercommandos died on that day.

Under the strict armed guard of the German soldiers, Samy stood with the other inmates watching the barbaric punishment meted out. He felt a total wave of depression engulf him as he began to think that there was no means to prevail over these brutal oppressors

The subsequent Nazi investigation into the use of explosives by the Sondercommandos traced the source of the supply, to a nearby munitions factory. Four Jewish women were suspected of having participated in the supply chain of the explosives and were arrested. Despite being brutally tortured, they refused to name any of their co-conspirators. Severely beaten, they were brought in front of the camp population and as an example to the other inmates, were publicly hanged.

Before her death one of the woman called out in Hebrew to her fellow inmates;

"Hazek Ve'ematz." - Be strong and have courage!

The destroyed Crematorium 4 was never rebuilt. In a small way, the brave rebellion by the Sondercommandos was able to slow down the killing machine of the Nazi SS.

For a short time after this uprising, the number of daily trains bringing new prisoners to Auschwitz began to decrease. Noticeably, fewer Jewish inmates were arriving at the concentration camp.

Samy believed that the reason for this occurrence was that many of the Jewish populations had already been wiped out. The reality was that this was only a temporary reprieve. International political pressure to stop the Nazis' persecution of Jews had resulted in a temporary cessation of the deportations.

Within a matter of a few days, the respite in policy was reversed.

The Nazis seized control of the Hungarian puppet government they had previously installed, on October 15th 1944. Despite all agreements to the contrary, the Germans now with complete dominance over Hungary, resumed the deportations of Jews to the concentration camps.

Elsewhere, the picture was different; the Nazis were losing ground and the war to the Allies. The Russian advances into Poland became a cause for concern for the Commanders of Auschwitz. The Nazis had vehemently denied the existence of their extermination camp practices as well as execution tactics. They did not want to get caught with the mountain of incriminating evidence in the event of an Allied capture of the concentration camp. The camp commanders surreptitiously began a process of evacuating inmates on departing trains to other concentration camps. The camps they were sent to were situated to the West and away from the advances of the Allies, such as Bergen-Belsen, Dachau and Buchenwald.

Over the following days and weeks, the Allied advances became a greater reality. However, for the inmates inside Auschwitz, unaware of the events external to their camp, life continued to be an unremitting place of suffering.

The temporary work Samy was selected to carry out varied on a regular basis. At this time, he was chosen to work in the woods. He and the prisoners had the task of collecting wood and loading them on to wagons. Instead of the use of horses, twenty prisoners were assigned to the task of pulling the loaded wagon filled with wood, back to the crematoriums.

Heavy snow had been falling and lay over a meter high on the ground. As Samy prepared to place a last load of wood on the wagon, he slipped into a pit of snow that covered a further meter of slush and icy water. Samy struggled to pull himself out, but become stuck in the mire, he did not have the strength to pull himself out. A fellow prisoner came to his assistance and helped to pull him out of the pit. In doing so, Samy's wooden clogs remained stuck at the bottom of the slush and he was unable to retrieve them. He huddled over from the bitter cold that overtook his body.

A German soldier had watched the incident, angrily, he came over and began to kick and use his fists to beat both Samy and the prisoner who had assisted the young boy. They were ordered to get back to their labor.

Samy continued to work for the rest of the day in the bitter cold. His stripped pajama clothing was wet and added to the iciness, his feet were bare and stinging from the cold of the snow, having lost his wooden clogs.

At the end of what had felt like an eternal day of work and suffering, Samy returned to his cellblock laager. He made an ineffective attempt to warm his frozen body and could not help falling into a state of complete depression.

Now weak and emaciated from the constant starvation, Samy decided that he'd had enough. He was tired of the daily horror of conveying corpses to the crematorium. His young eyes had seen things that adults hoped they would never see in a lifetime. He had experienced beatings and humiliation from the SS guards, for no reason other than their perverse amusement. Finally, he had lost hope of any salvation.

For the first time, Samy understood clearly the feeling of despair engulfing the inmates who had taken their own lives at the fences. He began to eye the temptation of throwing himself against the electrified fence and putting an end to his suffering.

Finally, later that night, Samy decided to take the walk of death. Slowly and deliberately, he walked out of the cell barracks. He looked up at the clearing skies, the snow clouds were dissipating and the stars were once more becoming visible. He took in a deep breath as he walked to steel himself for what he was about to do at the electrified fence. At the fence, he stared at the wire mesh for a few moments, and then he said a prayer. He raised his hands and moved them forward to grip the wire. Just before his fingers touched the fence, Samy paused. He remembered his father's words:

"Survive, so that one day you can tell the world what your eyes have seen."

Samy pulled back his hands at the last moment. He could not go through with the act of suicide. He turned, with his head hung low and shoulders drooped, he started to walk back to the cell barracks.

Nearby, there was a sudden flash of light followed by a scream of death, as one of the other inmates threw himself against the electrified wire and was electrocuted. Samy did not look back; he knew what had happened and, in a strange way, respected the courage of the man for having taken his destiny into his own hands.

Over the following days, still unaware of the Allied successes, Samy watched as fewer trains pulled into the railway siding.

The last train to arrive on October 28th, 1944 brought the final transport of Jews to be gassed at Auschwitz.

Two thousand Jews from Theresienstadt, on that train, were taken to the gas chambers and murdered. When the Sondercommandos had completed incinerating the bodies in the crematorium they too, were incarcerated, led to the gas chambers and executed. The murdered Sondercommandos were not replaced by new prisoners. The Nazis did not want to leave any witnesses alive to testify against them.

On October 30th, 1944, the inmates of Auschwitz saw the last use of the gas chambers with the carrying out of the execution of prisoners too weak or too ill to work.

Samy and his fellow inmates began to feel a glimmer of hope that with the gas chambers no longer utilized there would be a change in their captors' murderous policy. The Nazi killing fabric did not stop; it merely altered to the employment of bullets and the SS firing squads.

CHAPTER 11

THE RUSSIAN ARMY NEARS AUSCHWITZ

At Gestapo headquarters in Berlin, Heinrich Himmler, the founder and officer-in-charge of the Nazi concentration camps was keeping a very close watch of the Allied advances. He began to prepare to wipe out evidence of his command responsibility for the annihilation of Jews and groups the Nazis deemed unfit to live. Among the measures he took to cover up and avoid prosecution for the atrocities, was to order the destruction of the gas chambers at Auschwitz. On November 25th, 1944, the gas chambers of Auschwitz-Birkenau were blown up and destroyed in an attempt to conceal the Nazi crimes from the advancing Russian army.

Samy and the inmates of Auschwitz-Birkenau watched the SS guards blow up the hated structures, all the same, that brought little improvement to a life under constant threat of extermination. The German officers continued to carry out daily inspections of the barracks checking for inmates in bunks too weak or sick to work. Their clothes were taken away and the individuals marked to be shot the next day.

Samy had lived all his short life in the mild Mediterranean climate of Rhodes. The incoming winter activity began to turn even more bitterly cold. Samy, from his recent experiences, had already discovered that coping with brutally cold weather was an event he was totally unprepared for. The inmates were not provided with any warm clothing, they had to rely solely on their everyday prison garb for protection. At night, the prisoners would huddle together in the barracks around a simple stove for warmth. During the day, many worked barefoot in the blistering cold and snow. Samy was among those without shoes to protect his feet from injury by freezing and frostbite.

Many people died as the full winter cold set in.

The Russians achieved speedy advances in December against the Germans in the Eastern Theater of war. In response to the victories of the Red Army, and in the midst of the freezing temperatures of December, the evacuations of the Auschwitz inmates to other concentration camps increased. Trains became filled to capacity with prisoners being transported to western camp destinations.

The Nazis SS set three assumed objectives in attempting to clear the concentration camps. The first was that they did not want any of the incarcerated falling into the hands of the Allies to tell of the atrocities. The second was that the SS believed that they needed the slave labor prisoners to continue with their assembly lines of armaments at their western camps. The third objective was set purposely by Himmler himself. It was based on the premise that they would use the populations of the concentration camps as hostages to bargain for a peace and immunity from prosecution from the Allies.

The advances of the Red Army began to occur at a faster rate than the Nazis were able to cope with transporting the inmates out of Auschwitz. The Soviets liberated Budapest on January 6th, 1945, freeing eighty thousand Jews held by the Germans. On January 14th, the Soviets invaded Eastern Germany in their march against Berlin. A few days later, Warsaw, Poland was liberated on January, 17th and the Allies were within a few days marching distance of the concentration camps of Auschwitz.

The Nazi guards in order to secure cooperation of the inmates at Auschwitz deceitfully circulated rumors that the Russians intended to shoot all the prisoners found remaining at the camp.

Samy returned to his barracks after working in the fields one evening and overheard some of the inmates talking. Their conversation was about the "Rhodesli", a man from Rhodes who was lying recuperating from surgery in a nearby bunk. Eager to make contact with a person from his home island, Samy approached the bunk. He immediately recognized the man from Rhodes, as Giuseppe Cone.

Samy had known of Giuseppe on the island as a fellow member of La Juderia. He was much older at thirty-four years of age and a married man with three children. He saw that Giuseppe was lying painfully in the bunk with a large raw wound to his right leg. The wound was wrapped solely with toilet paper and oozing blood.

Samy had a rag-like blanket sitting over his shoulders for warmth; he took the blanket off and placed it on top of the bunk to cover the older man.

"I will stay by your side and look after you.' Samy offered, as he seated himself at the edge of the hard wooden bed.

The older man's pain filled expression changed briefly to a smile of gratitude, welcoming Samy's offer of camaraderie.

Despite the older man's agony, they instantly struck up a bond of kinship and talked about events that had befallen them since their deportations from Rhodes.

Giuseppe related to Samy that after their horrifying journey to Auschwitz, he had been separated from his wife and children upon their arrival. His young wife and children had avoided the gas chambers and been sent to do slave work at the Belsen camp. He had lost contact with them and did not know what had been their fate since that time.

He had been chosen to do slave labor at the coalmines. After having been quarantined, he'd had his head shaved, given rags full of bugs to wear, his arm was tattooed. Giuseppe looked down at his arm, where the number B-7251 had been imprinted. He almost robotically, spoke out the words of the numbers in German, those that he had to answer during the daily roll call:

"Swaing, zipson, ainon, fiftzin".

Giuseppe told Samy that his group of young men was transported to a place he believed was called, Riddertaou Charlotte Grubbe, a large coal mining area. There, he had been selected to work with other prisoners and technicians excavating coal and placing mine explosives.

Large rocks were needed as a support and to protect the jack for the gallery and wheeling for the tank containing the coal. He and the other forced labor worked inside the coalmine, hungry and cold and always in the dark carrying up those large rocks. They never experienced the sunlight or saw the daylight hours. They worked from early in the morning until late at night. They were continually overseen by shifts of SS units armed with sub-machine guns.

Due to carrying the extremely heavy weight of the rocks, Giuseppe developed a very large painful lump on his right leg. He had requested permission to go to the hospital for treatment. His request had been denied and was told that he could only receive treatment if he had a fever. The lump on his leg quickly became infested and he did in fact develop a fever. His skill at the mine was considered necessary; instead of being shot, he was permitted to go to the hospital.

Giuseppe had gone to the hospital that afternoon. A Jewish doctor who was a prisoner at the medical facility had operated on him without the benefit of anesthesia or proper medical instruments. The doctor had used a long stick and gauze. He had inserted and pushed the stick into his leg to draw out the infection. The primitive procedure had been, "very, very painful." Giuseppe explained.

Afterward, the doctor had used the only item available to protect the raw wound - he had wrapped toilet paper around the opening in his leg.

Exhausted and in pain, Giuseppe, closed his eyes and attempted to get some sleep, gradually, he slipped into a fatigued slumber. Samy curled up beside the man's bunk, closing his eyes, he too dozed into a light sleep.

Just before dawn, the SS guards entered the barracks to awaken the inmates for their workday.

One officer marched purposefully and deliberately to Giuseppe's bunk, shaking the sleeping man.

"Arbalt!" The officer barked in German, "To work!"

Painfully, Giuseppe lifted himself out of the bunk and proceeded to follow the officer out of the barracks back to the coalmine.

Samy watched Giuseppe agonizingly limp as he left the barracks. Blood was still seeping down his right leg as he walked. A sense of revulsion swept over him at the sight of the cruel treatment.

As the sands of time moved into January 1945, Samy turned fourteen years of age. His body had withered from malnutrition to a mere skeletal of skin and bones. He contemplated his situation and compared himself to a lighted candle where the flame were gradually eating away all the wax until there was nothing left to absorb - he was surprised to still be alive.

CHAPTER 12

THE DEATH MARCHES

During the first week of January, the same Nazi SS doctor who had wielded the enormous power of life and death by the mere movement of his finger to the left or right at the new arrivals in Auschwitz-Birkenau, did his rounds. This time he selected Samy and eight others inmates. They were immediately removed from their laager, marched to a separate building, and locked in a room containing ten individual beds with clean sheets. Samy and the others were told to lie on the clean beds and given orangeade and biscuits.

Samy and his fellow inmates were amazed and looked at each other in disbelief that this was actually happening. Desperately hungry, they took the food wondering what the reason was for the unusual attention they were receiving.

They soon found out a partial reason for the nourishment. The SS doctor and his assistants began to draw out a syringe full of blood from each of them; once in the morning, and once again in the evenings. Samy and his fellow inmates speculated what the SS doctor sought to do with "their Jewish blood". A few of the inmates believed that it was for experimentation. The others thought that the blood was to be used for transfusions to the German soldiers who were injured fighting the Russians, as the fighting got closer. The SS doctor never revealed to them the reason for taking their blood.

Just over a week later, the German commanders gave the order that the Birkenau sector of Auschwitz was to be evacuated to the main Auschwitz complex. The SS officers intended to blow up all evidence of the gas chambers and crematoria. They did not want to leave any trace of what had happened at the camp for the advancing Russians to find.

There were still in the region of 3,000 prisoners at Birkenau and the distance to the main camp was three kilometers. The prisoners were placed in columns of five people across and made to march under armed escort in quick-step through the bitter cold.

German soldiers with dogs and rifles were placed to the left and right, at the rear of the columns, soldiers marched with sub-machine guns. Any one falling out or unable to keep up with the march was to be executed. Shortly after the march commenced, the sub-machine guns of the SS soldiers began to open fire, killing those unable to keep up with the pace in the bitter cold.

One kilometer short of Auschwitz Samy staggered to keep up; he was totally exhausted and weak. Finally, he gave up and fell to the ground. Unable to carry on, he lay a few seconds in the snow and fully expected to hear a rifle shot giving him the *coup de grace*, ending his misery. At that moment, two prisoners wearing the same pin stripes and equally as emaciated as Samy, grabbed hold of him. One held him by the right arm the other by his left arm. They proceeded to pick him up off the ground and agonizingly dragged Samy along with them for that final kilometer to Auschwitz. Samy looked at the two men on either side of him. They were a little older than he was and he felt as though he was looking at the faces of two guardian angels. They were exerting all their energy to haul him along with them.

These two "angels" kept up their effort until they reached Auschwitz. Once there, they left Samy amongst the other inmates that had completed their journey. They did not wait for any thank you or gratitude, but simply walked away, having saved the young boy's life.

Samy wondered why those two had performed such a selfless act. In time, it had become the norm for each prisoner to treat his own preservation as paramount. There was little room through the hardships, malnourishment and inmate's lack of strength left to try to save anyone but one's own skin. Yet these two had reached out and saved him.

During the march from Birkenau to the Auschwitz main camp a full half of all the 3,000 that had started had been unable to keep up with the evacuation, and were all executed. If it had not been for the noble and selfless help of those two anonymous inmates, Samy knew he too, would have been among the ranks of those executed.

In the light of the inevitable Allied advance, camp guards took a final roll call on January 17th, 1945. There were still over sixty-seven thousand inmates remaining at the main Auschwitz concentration camp. The Nazis did not have the trains or trucks available to evacuate the prisoners before the advancing army would reach them.

Early the next morning in the midst of a heavy snowfall, the Nazis assembled the entire camp population. The Nazi Commanders announced that all of Auschwitz was to be evacuated that day. The prisoners were given a "choice". Either, of going on a fifty kilometer fast hike through two feet of snow to the border of the old German Reich, where they would be put on trains to other camps in or near Germany. Alternatively, those prisoners too weak or sick to take the trek could remain behind under the guard of their Nazi Polish surrogates and risk being "shot" by the advancing Russians.

Taken in by the deceit, sixty thousand prisoners chose to go with the Germans. Amongst them was Giuseppe Cone.

So, began one of the most notorious "Death Marches" of all time. In the bitter cold Polish weather, the SS guards commenced to assemble groups of inmates for the evacuation with rigid orders to shoot any prisoners who fell behind, were unable to walk, or lagged in any way.

In the darkness of the early morning, five hundred women and children from the main camp were placed into the first group to leave on the forced march. They were escorted out of the Auschwitz concentration camp by heavily armed SS troops. Phased in during the rest of the day they were followed by assembled groups of male prisoners under similar armed guard. They were force marched in the direction of Woodzislaw, Poland.

Next, they were followed by the prisoners from Monowitz and the sub camps. They were assembled and marched in the direction of Gleiwitz, near the German border with Poland.

Conditions of the forced marches through the bitter cold and snow were atrocious and prisoners were brutally mistreated. Following their precise orders, the SS guards shot scores of men, women and children too weak keep up with the march. There was no respite for anyone falling behind or being unable to continue, they were immediately executed. Prisoners suffered from starvation and exposure. Of those who were shot, their bodies were left lying along the sides of the roads.

The death toll escalated to a very high mortality count under the bitter conditions. Fifteen thousand of those souls taken from the camps died, or were executed along the way.

The first group of women arrived at Woodzislaw on January 21st, 1945. They were followed at regular intervals by waves of arrivals of the other escorted clusters of inmates, with the final group arriving the next evening.

The groups from Monowitz arrived at the four concentration camps of Gleiwitz on the same date. In the bitterly cold weather, they were split up and loaded onto open railroad cars of trains with different destinations. They headed to the concentration camps of Buchenwald, Dachau, Sachsenhausen or Mauthausen.

Giuseppe Cone was amongst those inmates that were grouped to go to the Mauthausen concentration camp, in Austria. Still suffering from his recent leg surgery, he had somehow survived the fifty-kilometer hike through the harsh weather. His group were loaded in open snow saturated cattle train cars and transported to their destination with snow still falling in a bitter cold environment. Conditions were so bad, that several more young men died during the transportation.

Upon their arrival in Mauthausen, Giuseppe observed the camp to be filled with a large number of arriving uniformed and non-military Russian prisoners. There was no place in the "Laager" - the shanty barracks - to accommodate the human cargo from Giuseppe's train. They were made to wait for their turn to be processed and for disinfection. They were forced to sleep for five days in the open and in the freezing cold. Many more prisoners unable to cope with the cold and hunger, died.

After processing, they were loaded back into the open cattle cars and taken by the train to the concentration camp in Ebensee.

Codenamed "Zement" by the Nazis for its secret research facilities, it nestled in upper Austria, in the mountains at the south end of Lake Traun. Despite its unique picturesque setting, Ebensee together with the Mauthausen sub camp of Gusen were regarded as the most horrific of the Nazi concentration camps.

The prisoners worked in twelve-hour shifts each twenty-four hour day. The camp at Ebensee provided slave labor for the construction of enormous underground tunnels for the housing of armaments. The original purpose of the tunnels was to accommodate the evacuated once top-secret Peenemunde V-2 rocket facility that had been bombed by the Allies. However, in July 1944, Hitler had ordered that the complex be converted into a tank gear factory.

Giuseppe and his co-workers arose at four-thirty in the morning and worked until six at night in those tunnels. Due to the design of the enormous apertures, they were often mistaken as opening into huge caves. The camp did not have sufficient facilities to accommodate the numbers of slave laborers; neither did it have a crematorium. Bodies were piled inside the few huts that had been built. Bodies were transported every third or fourth day to the crematorium at Mauthausen to be burned. The stench from rotting bodies of the dead, infested open wounds, urine and feces was overwhelming.

Giuseppe and his coworkers were issued with wooden clogs for their feet, when they fell apart they had to continue working barefoot. The camp was infested with lice and disease.

Their rations consisted of half a liter of coffee in the morning. Lunch at noon, consisted of three quarters of a liter of hot water containing potato peelings. Dinner was a 150 gram portion of stale bread. With insufficient nutrition to sustain the workers, the death toll continued to go up.

The mass evacuations from the other camps to the sub-camp of Ebensee put enormous pressure on the complex. There were twenty-five barracks that had been intended to house a hundred prisoners in each. With the continual arrival of new prisoners, they overflowed to housing seven hundred and fifty in each barrack. Many prisoners were made to dwell inside the tunnels, or, the less fortunate, outdoors in the open. From the proliferation to eighteen thousand inmates, hundreds died each day. The crematoriums were unable to keep pace with the number of bodies. Bodies were lined up and left outside the barracks. In an attempt to reduce the congestion, a ditch was built outside the camp and bodies were flung into quick lime. Giuseppe began to believe that each day of his survival was a miracle.

Giuseppe was assigned to unloading bricks from the arriving supply trains. The bricks were intended for the construction of more camp barracks for the prisoners. Despite their long work hours, the forced labor was unable to keep pace providing shelter for the increased arrival of human shipments from the cattle trains.

Giuseppe was also, sent to work in the tunnels where German technicians were conducting secret experiments into nuclear research. Giuseppe did not understand the use that the Germans made of this huge underground facility, but he observed that the tunnels were enormous structures that contained a complex of underground trains, tanks, and filled with a myriad of underground cables.

Food became further rationed to one daily slice of black bread and a cup of turnip soup. Hunger got the better part of Giuseppe and when the opportunity arose, he would chase the police guard dogs away from their meals and ate their dog food in order to survive. Consequently, Giuseppe developed dysentery and began to pass blood.

Because the Nazis needed skilled workers, he was sent to "Revir" – a hospital, to be cured. The hospital lacked adequate medicines. Without the proper treatment, Giuseppe needed to spend a month in the hospital confines recovering from his illness.

During his more lucid moments in the hospital, Giuseppe reflected on the fate of his wife and children. He prayed that they had somehow found a means to survive the horrors of the camps and were still alive. He also, reflected on young Samy, the thirteen-year-old boy whom he had met after his leg operation at Auschwitz. He wondered what his fellow Rhodesli had subsequently endured and what had become of him.

With the rush to evacuate Auschwitz, seven thousand five hundred prisoners were left behind. They were comprised mostly of inmates that the Nazis deemed too weak and sick to walk, or were dying and considered unfit to join the forced marches. They remained at Auschwitz under the guard of the Polish SS collaborators. Included in those numbers were a few who had hidden themselves among the piles of unburied corpses, to avoid being detected and taken on the forced marches.

Samy's body had become so emaciated that he been reduced to a walking skeleton, protected only by a thin layer of flesh. He was barely able to walk and very weak, he knew that he had no chance of survival on a forced march. He lay himself down amongst one of the many piled heaps of skeletons and decomposing dead bodies blending in with the dead, to avoid detection by the Nazis. In reality, he too, was very close to death. From this concealed place and with his eye vision dimming, he watched the events as they evolved around him at the encampment.

As the Germans evacuated, control of Auschwitz was taken over from the SS guards by the Polish militia raised by Hans Frank. He was a German Nazi lawyer whom Hitler had appointed as the head of the Government General of occupied Poland. The militias were left with the explicit instructions that in the event of the Allies imminent capture of Auschwitz to execute all the remaining prisoners. No one was to remain alive and there was to be no evidence left behind of the atrocities that had occurred at the concentration camps.

Samy, hidden within the confines of bodies, watched, as the remaining prisoners were kept sequestered inside of their barrack cells guarded by the Polish Militia. Movement outside and between the barracks was prohibited.

Sammy's young mind became confused with the situation. He had no idea of what was really happening or what was to become of him and the inmates that had been left behind by the Nazis. While not as ruthless as their Nazi masters, he could not understand why these Polish militias were keeping the remaining survivors confined to the barrack cells.

With the arrival on January 27th 1944 of The First Army of the Soviet Union on the outskirts of Auschwitz under the command of Marshall Koniev, the answers to all those questions became all too real and apparent.

The Polish militia prepared to flee, in the light of the imminent capture of the concentration camp. In accordance with their instructions to eliminate all survivors, they commenced to open fire and attack the barracks of the prisoners. The militia indiscriminately, began firing their automatic weapons and lobbed hand grenades into the buildings housing the groups of defenseless huddled inmates. Samy, helplessly, from his position amongst the pile of decomposing corpses watched the scene of total carnage take place around him.

A lobbed grenade landed close by inside a barrack, and Samy saw it burst and rip the inside of the building outwards. He heard the sounds of the screams and death wails of the weak and sick inmates that had been unable to get away to avoid the shrapnel from the explosion.

Samy, from his hidden position, watched as the Polish militiamen burst into barrack after barrack with rifles firing. A hail of bullets from their automatic weapons lethally sprayed into the buildings. The bullets splattered everywhere, mortally striking people. He saw a few of the men reach for grenades and hurl them into groups of inmates huddled for protection by their bunks. The resulting explosions destroyed the men and inanimate objects equally without distinction. Samy, in the middle of this carnage believed that the end of the world had finally arrived. He could not believe the slaughter that the Slaves were inflicting on the helpless captives.

Then, suddenly, the slaughter stopped.

The 332nd Rifle Division of the Red Army had advanced into Auschwitz and the Polish militia, unable to complete their mission, attempted to escape from the camp.

Samy heard a new sound of weapons fired. This time it was from a distance, as the Russians opened fire on the militia. The gunfire sounded louder as the two fighting forces came into closer contact with each other.

Several hundred inmates imprisoned in the barracks attempted to take the opportunity to escape. As they ran out in to the open, the Russians mistakenly thought they were a part of the fleeing militia and opened fire on the escaping prisoners, killing many of them.

Samy, frozen, nearly unconscious and terrified with fear remained in his hiding place amongst the dead. Too scared to venture a look at what was happening around him, he remained in that spot until finally, the shooting stopped.

An eerie silence of weapons no longer being fired fell over the concentration camp.

Men in uniforms that Samy had never seen before burst into view with rifles at the ready. Samy covered his hands over his head and closed his eyes tightly, not knowing what to expect next.

He could hear these uniformed men walking about the grounds and inspecting the barracks, talking in a language that was foreign to him.

The barracks and Auschwitz confinement area slowly filled with entering Russian combatants. As the soldiers commenced to walk around, taking in the sight of the sick, the emaciated, the wounded, the dying and the piles of the dead, many reacted with shock as though an emotional hammer had struck them.

Some of these battle hardened men responded to the excessiveness of the horrors they were seeing by breaking down in tears, while others unable to digest the atrocities in front of their eyes, dashed to an open place and threw up.

The Russian soldiers pressed forward, and continued to enter and comb the compounds that made up the concentration camps. While Samy could not understand what they were saying, his dimmed eyes watched their reactions.

From the startled expressions of shock on the soldiers' features, animated gestures and angered tone of their voices, it was evident that the soldiers were clearly astonished at the gruesome leftovers of the Nazi's atrocities.

A group of soldiers approached the heap of corpses where Samy had hidden himself. They stood in awe observing this evidence of the atrocities perpetrated at the concentration camp. The bodies, piled in heaps several corpses high, were located near a defunct crematorium. The mass of bodies piled there had lain and accumulated during the past week when the crematoria had not functioned. The stench of rotting corpses was overwhelming. Their shock heightened, when one of the soldiers noticed a movement from one of the bodies in the pile. On closer inspection, they saw the form of Samy; the young boy was scarcely breathing and barely conscious, but still alive.

On seeing that he was still living, the soldiers lifted Samy from his hiding place, and immediately called for transport to take him to a military hospital.

The soldiers continued to roam the different facilities taking in the remains of the gas chambers and the haphazard array of lifeless bodies left at the camp. The Russians immediately ordered that makeshift coffins be constructed and brought into the camp so that a burial could take place for the masses of dead. Bodies wherever possible were placed into an individual casket. A lengthy parade of Poles from nearby villages acted as bearers, carrying the caskets outside the concentration camp, for a burial in nearby fields.

Fewer than seven thousand prisoners had survived at the camp. For them it was a time of joy at being set free. For Samy, despite his condition, it felt like an amazing sensation to be free from the Nazi captors. For the first time, he cautiously looked about him without the oppressive feeling and presence of the Nazi sentries.

The soldiers placed Samy onto a transport to be taken to a small Russian military hospital that had been set up. As the transport moved out of Auschwitz it passed by large imposing metal gates at the entrance to the main concentration camp.

Looking up at the gated entrance he become aware of the Nazi words emblazoned in metal above the access as one entered. Now, at last able to let his youthful emotions out in the open, he feebly hunched his weak body and a tear streamed down his cheek.

The sign read; "Arbiet macht frei" – "Work makes you free!"

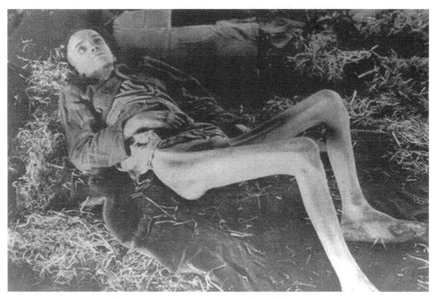

The young survivor the Russians found at Auschwitz
Source: http://www.itccolamonico.it/cosa-offriamo/progetti-pof/sami-modiano.html

CHAPTER 13

THE LIBERATION OF AUSCHWITZ

The surviving prisoners of Auschwitz were treated as "released" by the Russians. That treatment stood in stark contrast to the other concentration camps liberated by the British and American forces. In those concentration camps, the survivors continued to remain at the barracks as displaced persons and were looked after under the auspices of the British and American care.

The Russians having captured the concentration camp now simply released the prisoners. People, who had been brought to Auschwitz-Birkenau from a multitude of countries all over Europe, now had to fend for themselves. It was left up to them to find their way back to their homelands. Having accomplished their mission of liberating the Nazi camp, the Russians proceeded to push forward with their intended objective of an assault towards Berlin.

For the already emotionally scarred survivors, the euphoria of their new found freedom began to slowly evaporate into feelings of a sense of abandonment. Not knowing what to do next, the prisoners waited and wandered aimlessly for days at the Auschwitz barracks. Gradually, small pockets of the remaining survivors from twenty-nine diverse countries, took off on their own accord, through the freezing weather.

The harshness of the winter environment and their lack of adequate clothing to shield from the elements brought with it a sense of urgency for those remaining at Auschwitz. Desperate to find a means of food and shelter, some of the men, mostly with Italian nationality, volunteered to work collaborating with the Russians behind enemy lines. In return for their assistance with those allies, they received food, clothing and shelter among the Russian military laborers.

Samy, although in a very poor physical state found himself in the fortunate situation of having been transported by the Russians to a small military hospital for emergency care.

A female Russian doctor headed the hospital. This particular doctor took a warm and compassionate view of Samy because of his tender age and seriously weakened condition. She took him under her personal charge, using all available means to assist with Samy's treatment and to rehabilitate him.

Slowly and with the doctor's daily tender care, Samy's health and body began to recover. It took two months of treatment for Samy to regain sufficient strength to be fit to leave the hospital. He had been brought to the hospital on January 27th and it was now March 25th, 1945. The Russians were still very heavily involved in battles with the Germans as they pushed forward to take Berlin. Despite the Allied advances, the world was still at war.

With Samy having recovered sufficiently, the doctor who had done so much to help him, visited his bedside.

She told him in Russian "Robota!" "To work!"

She was in effect telling him that he now had to go to work assisting the Russian army.

Samy did as he was instructed by the doctor, and began to work, laboring with the other freed survivors from Auschwitz, as well as Russians. Their Russian counterparts accorded the former prisoners of Auschwitz treatment as equals. The military overseeing the work were engineering specialists, providing defenses for the army. Samy's duties consisted of helping to dig trenches in specific measurements of fifteen meters in length, one and one-tenth meters wide and one and one-tenth meters deep. The earth that they dug up was stacked to the left and right of the burrowed trenches to give extra cover above ground. Samy was told that the reason for the fox-holes was to provide a back up for the advancing Russian forces. Their armies were proceeding rapidly into German territory. The big fear was that their advancing armed forces were proceeding forward too speedily. In the event of a German counter attack, and the need arising for the Russians to retreat, they could fall back to the trenches. This would afford their soldiers a means of protection and allow them to regroup their forces and prepare for a second forward advance.

Samy and the other laborers worked at this exerting physical task every single day without a break for two months, until the end of the war.

Victory was at last achieved. Germany fell to the Russian and Allied forces. The end of the war in Europe was proclaimed during May 1945.

Samy and the other survivors of Auschwitz received the news with elation. They believed that they would finally be able to rest from the hard work endured during the past months.

They were allowed to rest for three days.

After the third day, the Russian military told the survivors that they now had to proceed to and work on a large river and lake, which they called the Roter. The German army had sabotaged the large river and lake's bridges during their retreat from the advancing Russian forces. The Auschwitz survivors and Russian workers were to be transported to perform labor on rebuilding the bridges and roads that had been blown up. They were told this was necessary now that the war was over to allow some of the Russian military contingent access to return home to Russia.

The Russians transported Samy and the laborers to a confined place by the river and put them to work repairing the bridge and roads. The laborers worked hard on repairing the access road and the main bridge over the river. The restoration work took a month to complete.

With that task completed, Samy and the other workers were taken to work on repairing a second bridge. This work took a further month to complete.

It was now August 1945. The war in Europe had been over for a couple of months, Samy and his fellow survivors from Auschwitz became very concerned about achieving their liberty. The war had ended and there was no freedom in sight for them.

Samy and the men rescued from Auschwitz met with the Russian officers. The Jewish leaders expressed their gratitude to the Russians for having saved them from the concentration camp. They went on to tell the officers that while they had voluntarily collaborated and worked with them, it was now post-war, and they all wanted to go home.

The Russian military officer in charge listened to their concerns and in response promised that they would be required to work for only one more week. He informed them that arrangements were in place for German laborers to be brought in to the site to continue with the work. He also, told them that after that week, they would be able to rest, and as they were Italian, transport would be made available to repatriate them to Italy.

In accordance with the agreement, Samy and the survivors continued to work for the Russians. The German laborers arrived as promised a week later and replaced them.

Samy and his group were told they would be leaving the encampment and were placed aboard a train and transported to the city of Cologne, in Germany. From there they were moved to a small town outside that city, by the name of Opel. The Russians had set up a large military base there. Samy's group was taken to the encampment and accommodated within the military confines. They were fed, clothed and housed at this facility.

The Russian officer-in charge informed Samy's group of survivors from Auschwitz, that while they were at the base, they would not be required to perform any labor. The officer explained that all the trains were full to capacity at this time carrying Russian military personnel to different staging points. He went on to tell them that in a short time, as soon as vacancies became available, they would be booked on those trains to travel back to Italy.

Samy and each of the members in his group of survivors were issued with documents, which declared that the named individual in that paper had collaborated with the Russian army and had assisted during the war. The document was to serve as a pass to allow them to travel freely in and out of the military base, as well as through Russian checkpoints in the town. These documents in time would become invaluable to Samy and the others, in their quest for freedom.

Samy and the survivors waited a week. They were not put on any of the departing trains. They waited a second week; again, they were not put on any trains leaving for Italy.

Samy now wanted desperately to leave this place. He had suffered through the anguish and misery of being orphaned and the loss of his little sister. He had endured the horrors of surviving the Auschwitz concentration camp. He had been deprived of an education when the Mussolini edicts had stopped him from attending the Italian schools on Rhodes. He thought of himself as being uneducated and ignorant. He craved to get back to some semblance of a reasonable life and clung to the solace of getting to Italy and the possibility of returning to his island of Rhodes.

During this time, Samy had struck up a friendship with a twenty-six year old co-worker and fellow Auschwitz survivor. He had come to rely on this man, twelve years his senior for guidance and advice. Lemantari was his name and he had originally come from Rome. During the war, Gestapo forces in Italy had chosen his father for random execution, while he had been selected for deportation from Rome to Auschwitz. Lemantari had been with Samy during much of their time at Auschwitz, and they had occasionally toiled together on assigned duties until the Russian liberation of the camp. After the liberation, Lemantari was amongst the Italians who had found themselves stranded in Poland and as a means of salvation had chosen to work for the Russians. Lemantari was in the work group Samy had been assigned to join after his recovery period in hospital. The two had subsequently worked together while collaborating with the Russian forces.

In contrast to Samy's lack of education and fourteen-year-old youthful naivety, Lemantari had been an academic and had been highly educated prior to his incarceration. He always watched and analyzed the events unfolding around them and took time to share his thoughts with the young boy. Samy looked up to him with respect and trusted this friend. They both waited anxiously with the others for the train to take them to Italy.

Lemantari, quietly watched, listened and studied what the Russians were doing as well as observing the train schedules. He discussed the situation with Samy, telling him that with all the trains departing he found it strange that a place had not been found for them on one travelling to Italy. He told Samy that things were not going as the Russians would have them believe and suggested that there was no intention of sending them back to Italy. Samy reacted with surprise, naively responding that they needed to wait and that the Russians would accommodate them on the next available train.

Lemantari shook his head in dissent, but agreed to wait two or three more days to see if there was any progress to send them back.

After three more days of waiting, there was still no hint of any travel arrangements to put them aboard a train traveling to Italy. Lemantari told Samy that they should prepare to escape from this place and Germany. He told Samy that he had spent time drawing up an itinerary and had drafted a route for them to take during their escape. He suggested that they should take flight the following night and leave by foot, walking to Italy. Samy naively, agreed with the older man's proposal. Lemantari then explained some details of his plan to the young boy to prepare them for the following night.

The next day, they secretly, collected as much food as they could carry with them and bundled a few items of clothing in a knapsack for their journey.

Lemantari had based his plan on the idea that they should travel under the cover of night and rest during the day. He proposed, that in instances where they were to cross any Russian checkpoints or were challenged, they would show their pass documents which stated that they had been Russian collaborators.

Accordingly, that night with the fall of darkness, they slipped out of the military camp and started walking. Samy had no idea of where they were and what distance they had to walk to achieve their freedom. He was completely reliant on Lemantari.

They walked and walked and walked, one day turned into two, then three days, then a week, two weeks, three weeks, always moving at night and resting during the day.

Samy would ask each day, "Are we close?"

Lemantari, would give the same optimistic answer each time, "Yes, just a little more distance and we will be there."

The decision to travel at night proved to be a blessing. The Russians for some reason had far fewer checkpoints set up during the dark. Lemantari and Samy presented their documents of collaboration each time they were confronted by the Russian authorities. They would nervously wait with baited breath while the soldiers checked their papers and silently exhale a sigh of relief when they were allowed to pass to the next control point.

When their food ran out, they would travel near houses that had gardens growing vegetables and fruit. Stealthily, they would enter the properties and steal crops growing there, eating such things as carrots, apples and grapes.

They always traveled by night and rested during the day. Lemantari, for all his intelligence was a man of very few words. Samy, to make up for the lack of conversation would look around him as they passed different scenery to keep his mind occupied.

As they walked, Samy would occasionally feel the chill of the night air.

The young boy would wrap his arms around his shoulders for some warmth. As they trekked, this open space, without boundaries, on occasion awed the young boy. Samy had become conditioned to the restrictions of the confines of a setting with overcrowded barracks, the threat of SS guards and electrified fences, he felt suddenly overwhelmed by the scenery he now experienced surrounding him.

Above, the twinkle of stars shone down and the moon made a bright appearance in-between a few clouds floating in the sky. Around Samy and his friend, the fields did not hold the constraint of military men, or, the threat of electrified fences. Instead, Samy saw an open view of scenery containing no repressive restraints, and for the moment, the deafening silence of quiet and tranquility.

He wondered, as they walked, if this was what peace looked like.

CHAPTER 14

THE LONG TREK DRAWS CLOSER TO FREEDOM

As Samy and his friend Lemantari trekked night after night slogging to make it out of Germany, Samy thought about the other Rhodeslis. He wondered about those who may have also survived the concentrations camps, and if they had survived, how were they faring with their own quest to salvage freedom.

Giuseppe Cone had endured several more months of the horrific nightmare, in the hands of the Nazis, at his location in Ebensee. His labor camp continued to operate and was functional until May 1945 when the Allied forces began to push forward and defeat the German positions in Austria.

The American advancing forces engaged the German army in close contact battles to come within reach of Ebensee in early May. Within days, they were able to liberate the concentration camp. Giuseppe was amazed at the cowardice of the previously arrogant and brash majority of SS guards, who simply laid down their weapons and took panicked flight. With the advancement of the Americans into the concentration camp, the residual SS guards surrendered and were captured.

After the liberation of the camp, Giuseppe, was sent by the Allied forces to a nearby hospital where weak, ill, and with swollen legs, he spent another month recuperating from his condition.

While he was convalescing at the hospital, Italian forces arrived. They were travelling in a convoy of trucks decked out with Italian flags. Their commander sent out word that they had come to repatriate their nationals and transport them back to Italy. While not fully recovered Giuseppe was eager to travel to a life of freedom and joined the repatriating convoy. The trucks set off via Innsbruck and Berzano. By the time the convoy reached Italy, Giuseppe was too ill to continue and was hospitalized once more in Modeno. After a few more weeks of medical treatment, the doctors diagnosed his condition sufficiently improved to travel. He was placed on varied modes of transport, comprised of trucks and trains, to Bologna, then Firenze and finally to Rome. There, he joined a few other young survivors of the concentration camps. They were all housed at a "Casa di Reposo" a home for rest, near the Italian seaside. With proper care and attention the boys were able over a course of several months to recuperate and recover their bodily strength.

Samy and Lemantari lost track of time as they trekked on during their journey. They estimated that they had been walking close to a month and a half. Finally, one night they came within sight of the German border with Austria. Hardly believing their eyes, tears of relief streamed down their faces as they approached the frontier.

The Austrian border post was being manned by the Allies, mainly American soldiers.

As Samy and Lemantari came closer to the post, they were challenged by the frontier soldiers. The militia was astonished when Lemantari explained that he and Samy were Jewish survivors of Auschwitz and that they had walked all the way from Cologne to this Austrian frontier. The Americans offered them their assistance, inquiring what their intended destination was. When Lemantari explained that they were Italian nationals and hoped to reach Rome, the American soldier in command, gave them a simple answer:

"Okay, no problem!"

That night they were housed in American barracks, given new clothing and at last able to take a refreshing bath.

The following day, they were transported to the train station where they met and were grouped with other former war prisoners and militia. They were placed aboard a train and taken to the Italian frontier. From there they were put aboard trains that made several stops, sometimes for an entire day, sometimes for six or seven hours along the journey. Lemantari and Samy found no cause to complain at this slow progress and were grateful no longer to be walking. After a week, they finally arrived in Rome during the night.

They were assembled before a group of Italian military officials posted at the train station to meet repatriating nationals.

The Italian officials interviewed Lemantari. After listening to his description of the events, they concluded that as he lived in Rome, there was nothing further they could do to assist him, he was "home" and instructed him to proceed to his family residence.

Turning their attention to the young boy, the officials appeared perplexed as to what to do with him. Lemantari interceded; explaining that Samy had lost his parents and family at Auschwitz and now had nowhere to go. The boy had been taken from Rhodes Island and wished to return there. Lemantari urged the officials to allow Samy to stay in Rome for a little while until word could be conveyed to their superiors that the boy was without any family and destitute and to ask them do something to assist him

The officials made notes of Samy's circumstances and issued him with a document. He was told to present himself at an address specified in the paper. Samy was informed that at this place there would be food, a bed to sleep, doctors present to check on his health and he would be provided with any needed treatment.

Having accomplished this status for Samy, Lemantari interceded once more, he told the military officials that he wanted to take Samy with him to his home for a few days. He wanted to introduce Samy to his mother and sisters and for him to rest at his home. He offered to take Samy after those few days to the place the officials had designated for him to stay.

The Italian officials agreed to allow this arrangement and Samy accompanied Lemantari to his home in Rome. The event was a wonderful and heartbreaking homecoming for Lemantari, as he was greeted and reunited with his mother and two sisters at their home in Rome. For Samy, it turned into a strange and emotional sensation to be inside a family home once more and to experience the momentary taste of family life.

The following day, Lemantari took Samy with him to a location in Rome where his father had been executed. It was a bombed out cave area where a monument was earmarked to be erected to Jews who had died as martyrs. As Lemantari paid tribute at this place, his eyes filled with tears, and he related to Samy what had happened to his father and other innocents at this place. He explained that in 1944 Italian partisans had carried out an act of sabotage against the Nazis, killing thirty Gestapo soldiers. In retaliation, the Nazis had ordered that the persons responsible were to surrender themselves to the Nazi authorities or the entire community would suffer. They announced that if the persons responsible did not give themselves up within a period of one week, ten people would randomly be selected for each German soldier that had died. There would be a mass execution of those random civilians if the guilty partisans did not surrender in compliance with this order. The perpetrators of the sabotage did not have the courage to give themselves up. The Germans randomly selected three hundred Italians half of whom were from the Jewish community; one of them was Lemantari's father. Those innocents had been marched to this cave and sealed inside. The Germans then proceeded to place explosives within the cave among those chosen civilians. The explosives were detonated and all three hundred inside the cave, including Lemantari's father, had perished.

Samy spent a few days with this family. Lemantari then assisted him to find the "Casa di Reposo" which the Italian authorities had designated to be his temporary home. He was fed, clothed and housed at this facility. Samy was examined by doctors and they determined that while he had recovered physically, because of his tender years he needed psychological help to overcome the loss of his family and mental horrors that he had experienced. He was sent to a clinic in Ostia, outside Rome where he underwent mental treatment for a period of two months.

While at this clinic in Ostia, Samy met up with Giuseppe Cone and eight other young survivors from Rhodes. Being with fellow Rhodeslis helped with much of the healing process and they joined in many activities together. They also set about the endeavor of finding relatives who were still alive in the different countries around the world. They were gradually, each able to make contact with relatives who had left Rhodes Island prior to the war years and deportations. Those relatives offered the children to come and join them in the new countries that they now considered their home.

During his time at the rest home, Giuseppe Cone considered his options and realized like his fellow survivors from Rhodes, that there was nothing left on his former island to encourage him to return home.

Giuseppe immigrated to the Belgian Congo and settled in the town of Elisabethville in the Katanga province. He lived there for a period of twenty years until conditions deteriorated in that African country, which went through the political upheaval of a civil war. Giuseppe fled to South Africa as a refugee and lived out the rest of his life in the beautiful city of Cape Town.

He rarely talked of his nightmare experience until late in his lifetime. When he was eighty years old, he drafted a public document, writing to all who would be interested in learning of the history of the Holocaust,

"I hope that you will always continue to let the world know of the damage – injury – detriment that we have suffered."

During the months of April and May 1945, British and American forces were also able to liberate a total of six young teenage girls of Rhodes Island from the remaining concentration camps. The young "Rhodeslis" were transported by train to Italy. In Bologna, the girls met up with and were cared for at the military barracks by British soldiers of the Jewish Brigade from Palestine.

CHAPTER 15

TURKISH JEWS AND THE AFTERMATH ON RHODES ISLAND

The deportation of Rhodes' Jewish population to the Auschwitz concentration camp left a barren void on the island's Jewish quarter. All that was left of that once thriving island community were the forty-two "Turkish Jewish" people saved by the actions of the Turkish Consul-General, Selahattin Ulkumen. For those who had been deported, their houses, property and possessions in the quarter were slowly appropriated and taken over by the local Greek population.

A short time after the Jewish deportations, Turkey renounced its neutrality, that country sided with the Allies and declared war on the German Axis. In defiance of the established international conventional norms of diplomatic immunity, the Nazis arrested Selahattin Ulkumen in Rhodes. He was placed aboard a freighter taken to Athens, and jailed in Piraeus for the rest of the war.

The remaining forty-two Jewish people on learning what had happened were distressed by the arrest of Ulkumen. They saw in him a brave savior and with his removal, the loss of the man who had been so vigorous in protecting them. During the following months, the Jewish Turks were subjected to harassment, detention for lengthy periods, as well as the constant threat of deportation.

Some of the Jewish families had earlier, been able to move to nearby villages to be away from the city center and from the bombings.

One of those families was the Turiel family.

Daniel Turiel was married with two young children, Boaz and Elliot. His family had been merchants on the island for decades and owned an old and small farm in a village about twelve kilometers from Rhodes City. Alarmed by the events and bombing in La Juderia, Daniel decided to move the family to that nearby village. Transportation out of La Juderia was difficult to procure, but he was able to arrange for a horse and cart to take the family and some of their possessions to the small farm.

The old property did not have a house with living facilities. Daniel had employed a local Turkish farmer, Abidin, as a caretaker for the farm. The local man was, also, a good friend of the family. Unannounced, Daniel and his family proceeded to show up at the home of this adjoining farmer. Abidin, despite himself having meager living facilities for his own family, welcomed them into his home. He emptied out one of his tiny rooms, laid down a mattress and welcomed the Turiel family to spend as much time as they needed with his family.

During the following months, the Turiel family was always made to feel welcome at the humble homestead. The children learned to cultivate the fields; they carried out customary farming duties such as picking the fruit and nuts from the trees and joined Abidin's sons in both work and play. There was a true sense of each becoming a part of the other's family.

Owing to the onerous reporting conditions imposed on them by the Nazis, the Turiel family moved back into the city. For the sake of group safety, the family moved into an apartment complex in the new section, living together with the other Turkish Jews that had been saved from the deportations.

The Nazi commanders of Rhodes had begun to formulate plans to deport the remaining Jewish families. However, that planning was soon abandoned as the Allies began to take control of the Aegean Sea. The Third Reich was falling into disorder and Rhodes' Nazis became more concerned with saving themselves than harming and deporting the remaining Jewish families.

During October 1944, it became apparent to the Gestapo commanders on Rhodes that the tide of war had clearly turned against them. More out of a desire to rid themselves of evidence of the atrocities they had committed on the island, the Jewish families were told they could leave for Turkey. They were placed in a crowded, large, sailboat to make the journey to the Turkish mainland.

Shortly after the sailboat set out to make the crossing, the families encountered unfavorable wind conditions, which forced them to return to Rhodes. Upon their return to the port, the Turiel and other families aboard the sailboat discovered that their vessel had a bad leak. Had they continued on with the voyage the crowded boat would have sunk and the families aboard would likely have perished in the sea. There was no other available means of transport to take them off the island. As a result, they remained on Rhodes for a few more months until January 1945.

In early January 1945, the German commander was informed that representatives of the International Red Cross were to visit Rhodes to look into the state of affairs of its population. The Nazis in order to avoid the very damaging testimony the Jewish families would have as to their treatment, ordered the remaining Jews to go to Turkey. The next day, at dawn, the families were all crowded aboard a sailboat and embarked on a several hour journey across stormy seas. It was a treacherous and hard voyage for the families and they finally arrived at Marmaris, Turkey, late that night.

The Turiel family, despite the hazardous journey gratefully embraced their landing on Turkish soil. After a short stay of a few days in Marmaris, the family continued on to Izmir. There, they stayed with relatives until their departure for New York City and the United States in July 1946.

With the unconditional surrender of the Third Reich, in 1945 and the end of the war in Europe, the Germans vacated the Island of Rhodes. The Allies replaced the Germans on the island and the Greeks took over the administration of the Dodecanese.

Of the once thriving and bustling two thousand Jewish members of La Juderia, only a hundred-fifty-one members had survived the deportation and atrocities of the concentration camps. Most were in very poor shape physically and needed to spend months recovering from their ordeals, housed in Italian and refugee centers of Europe.

The surviving leaders of La Juderia returned to Rhodes at the conclusion of the war and took with them the flicker of a flame; the hope of resuscitating the old Jewish Quarter. They brought with them the memories of the richness of a life, warmth and happiness that had been so much a character of La Juderia.

What they found upon their return to their formerly well-known surroundings was desolation. The once familiar faces, that had sat outside their time worn doorsteps, greeting passersby's, smiling, laughing and engaging in conversation, were all gone. There were no Jews left on Rhodes. They laid a wreath at an old fountain adorned with three metal seahorse statues set in the center square of La Juderia, in memory of all those that had perished.

The leaders proceeded to meet with the Turkish Grand Mufti of Rhodes, Seyh Suleyman Kasilioglu. He took them to his mosque and retrieved from the pulpit of the Morad Reis, the precious collection of the Torahs of La Juderia. Included among them, was the several-hundred-year-old Torah that he had so carefully secreted from the Nazis. The Jewish leaders gratefully took possession of the precious scrolls and returned the Torahs to their rightful places inside the ark at the Kahal Shalom synagogue on Dossiadou Street.

CHAPTER 16

RETURN TO RHODES AND THE NEXT GENERATION

One hundred and fifty-one of the former Jewish inhabitants of La Juderia had one way or another survived the horror and atrocities of the concentration camps. Forty of them, returned to Rhodes to what they thought were their homes after the war. However, for them the nightmare was not over. What they found was that some of the local Greeks had taken over their homes and what had remained of their possessions.

The Greeks denied responsibility for the deportations and offered no compensation for the property and possessions. Before the war, relations between the Greek and Jewish communities were good and many personal friendships had flourished. However, since the German occupation and the deportation of the community from La Juderia, a new situation faced those who returned. Apart from problems with their homes and belongings, the returning members of La Juderia were confronted with one more major factor. The life that they had once known, no longer existed. Instead of a joyful return to their beautiful island, they were faced with the heart wrenching memories of the life they once had being replaced by reminders everywhere of the atrocity that had all but wiped out the population of La Juderia.

The conditions on their return to Rhodes for most became overwhelming, and many left a short time later to join relatives and friends, settling in other parts of the world. Those that embarked in trying to recover their homes, found themselves embroiled in legal court actions trying to establish their rights to the usurped properties. Some cases dragged on for years, with the last action being settled fifty years later in 1995.

Violette Fintz was one of those survivors who returned to Rhodes. She had been liberated from the concentration camp on April, 15th 1945. She had returned to the island in the hope of regaining her former position as the manager of the Singer Sewing Machine Company. On her arrival, she discovered her home had been ransacked. After resuming her job, she would seldom venture into La Juderia. The memories everywhere of her family and friends that had perished became overpowering on her emotions and left her in tears. After a year of attempting to endure and exist with the constant recollections and reminders of what had occurred in La Juderia, she too left Rhodes. She immigrated to the Congo to join her sister, and settled in that country.

Her story turned into a microcosmic reflection of the situations faced by all the deportees of La Juderia who tried to return home after the war. The Greeks now occupied **most of** their homes and Jews on the island were a rarity. The once bustling synagogue, Kahal Shalom struggled to find ten people to attend services. Ten is the minimum number of men required to form a quorum (a minyan) and to say the Kaddish prayers for the dead.

The remaining number of the survivors who did not return to Rhodes Island moved on to other countries once they were fit enough to leave their refugee camps. They joined family, relatives and friends who had left Rhodes prior to the Nazi invasion of the island and the Holocaust. Some moved toward the open arms of those Rhodeslis living in the United States, and who had established themselves in the communities of Atlanta, New York, Seattle and Los Angeles. Others traveled to Buenos Aires, in South America. The new congregations emerging in the African countries of the Belgian Congo, and British Southern Rhodesia, also welcomed them.

Samy's choice, once he was fit to travel, was to travel and establish himself in the Belgian Congo.

Though the population of La Juderia had effectively been wiped out, the generation that had been fortunate to leave the island prior to the Second World War, indelibly, and with heartbreak, remembered them. While most of those émigrés had now begun to flourish in their new homelands, all had had a family member, relative, or close friend that had been killed by the Nazi deportations on the island of Rhodes during the Holocaust.

Isaac and Djoya Hanan had perished during the war along with their daughter Allegra. Their surviving children all did well as the years passed. Morris, their eldest son, had left for America at the age of thirteen to seek his fortune and send money back to assist the family. He had gradually made his way to Seattle where he started a tiny sidewalk enterprise selling shoelaces at the world famous Pike Street Market on the wharf. In time, he grew to own several businesses at the market and became a part owner of that landmark property. He expanded as well, to own several waterfront buildings and an apartment complex. Two of the sisters Mathilda and Serena followed Morris, married men from Rhodes and owned vegetable store outlets at the Pike Street Market.

Leon, the second eldest son who also left Rhodes at a very young age saw service during the Second World War with the United States military. He was lightly wounded while serving in Italy. He lived in Los Angeles reaching the age of one hundred. Rita married Robert Benveniste, a doctor, also from Rhodes, and they settled in Beverly Hills.

The two siblings, who went to Southern Rhodesia in Africa, flourished. Raphael returned briefly to Rhodes some years before the war to marry a lady from the island; Djoya. Together, they returned to set up home in Africa. Raphael started a furniture factory, which over time grew and expanded into a sizeable enterprise with the added expertise of their two sons.

Victor and Rachel Benatar started a farming venture early in the history of the emerging Southern Rhodesian countryside and later moved to the capital city of Salisbury. They had three children. In Salisbury, Victor and Rachel opened a bicycle business. In time with the energy of their eldest son Sam, the business grew into a wholesale, assembly and distributorship of bicycles. The middle child, Louise, was a gifted dancer and continued a lifelong friendship with Margaret Redfern, daughter of the decorated British Captain who was killed during active service in the Aegean.

Their youngest son, Isaac, was named after Isaac Hanan, the grandfather who was killed on the train journey from Athens to Auschwitz. This youngest sibling went on to graduate from the University of London with a law degree and became an author of several books. And, yes, that is me, recounting the events of Rhodes and the Holocaust so that we may "Never forget".

For Samy, having survived the atrocities of Auschwitz, his story continued into adulthood. He spent two years in Italy receiving medical and psychological treatments to help him fully recover his body and mental state from the loss of his family and atrocities witnessed. During that time, he began to understand like the others, that there was nothing left for him to return to in Rhodes. His inquiries led to him finding an uncle living in Africa and Samy decided to join him. Samy traveled to the Belgian Congo, where over time he set up business as a merchant. Like many of the others who had suffered the atrocities and experienced the mind numbing dread of the concentration camps, he spoke little of the ordeal he had gone through. Instead, he and the others attempted to settle in to what would be the closest to a "normal life".

Samy did not return to Rhodes Island until ten years later, during December of 1954, when he was twenty-four years old. He like the other Jewish population of La Juderia that had been deported all possessed the prewar Italian nationality. The Island was now no longer an Italian territory and had been handed over by the Allies to Greek sovereignty.

Not having Greek nationality made it difficult for any former resident to return and live in Rhodes. Samy however, stayed on the island for a month and while there successfully staked a claim for the return of his parents home. During that time, he visited the old and familiar landmarks he had known as a child. He experienced a sense of comfort when he observed that while badly damaged by bombs, the walls of the Kahal Grande, the great synagogue, and the Alliance Israelite School were both still standing.

However, when he returned for the second time eight years later in 1962, they had both been flattened. The walls of the Kahal Grande had been knocked down and the property stood as a ruin with solely the stone-decorated floors left intact. The dedication fountain and plaque to the Alliance Israelite School was now the only remnant left that a Jewish school had once existed there.

The oldest synagogue, the Kahal Shalom, still stood and remained intact though in need of restoration and renovation. The descendants of La Juderia aware of the temple's significance paid their respects at this place of worship during their future visits to Rhodes. However, most visitors traveling to this now increasingly popular Mediterranean resort walked the street unaware of the synagogue's unique history and significance. There was nothing provided to inform them of the past and the distinctiveness of the Temple.

A lawyer from Los Angeles and a descendant of a family from La Juderia, Aron Hasson, visited Rhodes in 1995 for a family reunion. During his visit, he perceived the lack of historical information about the Jewish quarter. Aron concluded that while much of the remnants of the Jewish life no longer existed because of the Holocaust, it was important to publish an informational pamphlet for future generations. Two years later, he founded the Jewish Museum of Rhodes to further that goal.

Two institutions were established in1997. Firstly, was the Rhodes Jewish Museum with a display of photographs donated by descendants of the Rhodeslis from around the world. Secondly, Aron set up the Rhodes Jewish Historical Foundation, a nonprofit organization to further the goals of the museum. A web site was also created with visual effects depicting the life of La Juderia.

Over time, work has progressed in enlarging and improving the building and contents at the Jewish Museum of Rhodes at the Kahal Shalom synagogue.

The work on adding donated exhibits and the renovation projects to the building has been an ongoing process that has stretched over many years. In 2004, a major restoration process over a period of two years was undertaken.

In 2006, the restoration of four additional rooms adjoining the Kahal Shalom was completed providing repairs to the roof, new doors and windows. The exhibit of artifacts, including a Torah hundreds of years old was put on display.

During July 2009, the Jewish Community of Rhodes unveiled the "Book of Memory", containing a list of names of each individual victim from Rhodes and Cos. The book is situated in the courtyard of the Kahal Shalom synagogue on permanent display, and in memory of the once vibrant community of La Juderia. It is a reminder "never to forget" the events that took place on the Island.

Samy's saga continued beyond his relocation to Africa. After many years of residing in his new country, the Belgian Congo was granted independence and which very quickly degraded into a state of civil war. Samy left the Congo and settled in Italy, in a beach community just outside Rome.

In 2004, Samy, after several years of holding within him his terrible memories and his family losses, began to talk openly about his experiences. He became a regular lecturer on the events of the Holocaust. He was interviewed by TV stations and the media, where he talked and shared the facts of his childhood during the war. Spending much of the summer months in Rhodes, he gives frequent talks at the restored Kahal Shalom synagogue to tourists, visitors and the descendants of La Juderia who make a pilgrimage to that sixteenth century place of worship.

Having been taken as a thirteen year old by the Nazis to Auschwitz and the ensuing course of events, Samy had not been able as a boy, to celebrate his Barmitzvah. That situation was put right in January 2007, at the Great Synagogue of Rome, when Samy, at last, celebrated his Barmitzvah in front of a congregation of hundreds of well-wishers. Samy turned seventy-eight that year. With tears in his eyes after reading from the Torah, he thanked the community for being with him at that very special occasion.

The ceremony was presided over and honored by the presence of the Chief Rabbi of Rome, Riccardo DiSgni. As the Rabbi continued with the ceremony, he watched Samy unwrap the sleeve of his left arm to fold the Tefillin binding around the arm (Traditional black leather boxes containing scrolls of parchment inscribed with verses from the Bible). There was a very poignant moment as Samy, in doing so, exposed the Auschwitz concentration camp tattoo number; B-7456 that was permanently inscribed into his flesh.

CHAPTER 17

LA JUDERIA LIVES ON

Samy continues to travel and reside in Rhodes during each of the busy summer tourist months. While there, he devotes much of his time on the island to the Kahal Shalom synagogue, giving regular lectures and speaking about his Holocaust experiences to visitors at the temple.

Rhodes has retained much of its medieval beauty and since the war years has increasingly become popular as a world tourist destination. Large cruise ships conducting tours of the Greek islands frequently use the deepwater pier two hundred yards from what was once La Juderia, as a port-of-call.

Located in the heart of the former Jewish Quarter today is the "Square of the Martyred Jews" (Martyron Evreon, in Greek). This is where Djoya and Allegra Hanan, as well as eleven other residents of La Juderia, were killed by dropped bombs during Passover of 1944. It originally contained Jewish homes and small shops. The destroyed buildings were not rebuilt, and in their place a small park and square has been established.

In 2002 as a result of several years of planning by the Greek government in collaboration with the Jewish Community of Rhodes, a Holocaust Memorial was erected in the "Square of the Martyred Jews." The dedication on a six sided black granite column is in memory of the World War Two victims from Rhodes and the island of Cos. Each of the sides is inscribed in a different language: Greek, Hebrew, English, French, Italian and Ladino. The memorial has the words engraved: "IN ETERNAL MEMORY OF THE 1604 JEWISH MARTYRS OF RHODES AND COS WHO WERE MURDERED IN NAZI DEATH CAMPS. JULY 23, 1944."

Today, there are only in the region of thirty-five Jews living in Rhodes. Though, many of the descendants of La Juderia, aware of their history, make their way to visit this ancestral homeland.

In August 2007, I traveled to Rhodes to pay my respects at the gravesites of my grandparents and aunt. I also did a daily pilgrimage to the Kahal Shalom synagogue the old and lone surviving temple of the Jewish quarter.

In front of the synagogue there is a plaque containing the family names of those who perished as a result of the Holocaust. I stood in front of the plaque and reached to touch the inscribed names of "Hanan" and "Benatar". Tears welled up in my eyes as I stood there and became lost in thoughts of those victims.

From behind, I heard a voice addressing me; posing a question in Judeo-Spanish:

"Did you lose some members of your family members to the Holocaust?"

I turned around and noticed that the voice had come from an elderly man perched nearby on a three-foot high brick veranda wall.

I answered him; 'Yes, my last name is Benatar, and my mother's maiden name was Hanan."

He introduced himself to me simply, as "Samy".

I observed that he was about six foot tall, well proportioned, and had a heavily sun-tanned face with grey hair. He looked remarkably fit and in good physical shape for a man of older years. We chatted for a little while and I enjoyed conversing with him in the Judeo-Spanish language. He pointed to a posting of a list of events for the synagogue that day and mentioned that he was scheduled to give a lecture about the Holocaust.

At the synagogue, I listened in to his lecture as one of the few survivors of the Holocaust from Rhodes. He explained that it was only now in his later years, that he was emotionally able to open up and talk publicly of his experiences and his deportation to Auschwitz as a thirteen-year-old boy.

Tears poured from my eyes as I listened to him tell of his life on Rhodes. He started his lecture explaining how, during the war, he had lost his mother to illness, due to a lack of available medications. He went on to detail the Nazi's efforts to wipe out the entire community of La Juderia by rounding up the Jewish community, including him, his eleven-year-old sister and his father. He went on to explain the deceit employed in the preparation, imprisonment and subsequent deportation of the entire Jewish community to a concentration camp.

I stayed on the island for an additional ten days and visited the synagogue daily. Samy was always there and we got to converse on a regular basis in Ladino. He was proficient in French and Italian, but spoke very little English. I could never hear enough of the stories of La Juderia. I wanted to learn more from him and the others at the synagogue of the events that had overcome this once thriving Jewish quarter. Consequently, the seeds were born to write this story of the events. I began to research, retrace and visit the places that were once part of the communal life of La Juderia

For me, perhaps this book has been the fulfillment of a comment made by my grandfather Isaac Hanan on a rainy Purim night in March 1944, when the Turkish messenger delivered a letter and the news of their new grandson.

"Perhaps when my new grandson and namesake, Isaac, becomes a man, he will learn what we endured, know of our experiences, and tell the world."

In the years subsequent to the war, the former Turkish Consul-General of Rhodes, Selahattin Ulkumen, has been honored and his deeds documented by both the descendants of the Jewish families of Rhodes and by the State of Israel. His bravery in standing up to the Nazis and saving forty-two precious lives is etched into the annals of "La Juderia".

My mother Rachel and aunt Mathilda also, in later years traveled to Rhodes to revisit the place of their birth. While on the island, they went on a nostalgic visit to their former childhood home. As they approached the residence formerly occupied by their parents Isaac and Djoya Hanan with their brothers and sisters, they saw the entrance door wide open and a Greek woman sweeping the floor outside. Through the open doorway they were able to observe the same table and furniture that had belonged to their family when they had lived there as children. They approached the woman sweeping outside the house and explained why they were there and that they would appreciate being allowed to see the inside of their former home. They told her that they had no intention of making any claim to the property but merely wanted to visit the inside of their childhood home. On learning who they were, the women shut the door, barring them from seeing anything further, and refused them entry.

Rhodes Island continues to be a jewel of the Mediterranean islands and each year Samy will continue to return as long as he can to the Kahal Shalom to give his lectures.

In an interview during July of 2009, Samy recorded the following comments.

"I have occupied my later years to a great extent to the Kahal Shalom, as I consider it to be my obligation. I hear the voices of the two thousand Jews who are now in the heavens saying to me "Samy, we left you behind on earth, but why did we leave you behind? Because you are a testimonial to what happened to us!"

"I will say things that you will not comprehend, no one, without going through what I have, can understand those feelings. It is how my mother died, my father and little sister died, how all those who perished at Auschwitz-Birkenau died, especially in the horror at that concentration camp. I too had put myself in front of death. I looked for death as a form of liberation from that torment, because death would have put an end to the suffering. I perceived each time I came before death, a feeling that it was not my time to die and death would turn me back. I would experience that confrontation almost daily, because at Auschwitz-Birkenau death was a form of liberation. For some of us, we would go in search of death and for those that did not find it; the electrified fence was ultimately a way of achieving that goal. That emotion is something, which is very difficult for most to comprehend.

"When the Russians came to liberate us, I was fourteen years old. They found me lying in with the heaps of the dead. Had the Nazis been aware that I was still alive they would have killed me. They did not want to leave any living being behind to give testimony to their atrocities.

"When I saw the face of the first Russian soldier I did not recognize who or what he embodied. Instead, I saw the face of my father, mother, my little sister and the two thousand of us that regarded each other as members of a family that were no more. They were faces of people from Rhodes who all knew each other and were close knit in customs and traditions.

"The almighty gave me continued life and when I question why he has kept me alive; the answer is that it is to give this testimony at the Kahal Shalom of the events that befell us.

"In these my final years I have worked hard to pass on my testimony, I do it with great contentment, because the message goes out to the future generation; the children. Their interest gives me a positive feedback and the strength to continue.

"Every winter, I accompany three hundred students from Italy to Auschwitz-Birkenau, so that they can see and learn what happened there. They begin to understand the pain and suffering that occurred there. For me each return that I make to that place is painful, but I do it because I believe something positive will come from it. The students travel to Auschwitz-Birkenau with me, a person who suffered there and that allows them to understand better what occurred. I point out places where I worked, where I slept, the crematoria, the place where cruel tests was performed on children, the place where women were experimented on, where bodies were heaped and the electrified fences. When children have this explained first hand by a survivor, they do not forget.

"I will continue to come here each year that the Almighty keeps me alive!"

"Never Forget!"

Historical map drawing; showing the castle-fortress city of Rhodes Island and La Juderia

Source: Rhodes Historical Foundation

THE HANAN FAMILY: Left to right, children Rita, Serena, Raphael, father Isaac,
mother Djoya holding baby Allegra, Salvatore, Mathilda and Rachel

Source: Benatar/Hanan Family photos

Allegra Hanan
Source: Benatar/Hanan Family Photos

1935 photo of the wedding of Daniel Behor Israel and Julia Hasson. This is the procession down "La Calle Ancha" of the wedding ceremony.

Source: Rhodes Historical Foundation

German tanks outside St. Catherine's Gate in 1944. Photo from Jo Mallel.
Source: Rhodes Historical Foundation

1943 photo of a young Rhodian Jewish boy, Alexander Angel, wearing the Star of David on the lapel of his coat. The Jews of Rhodes were not required to wear the Star. For the photo he is wearing the star as an innocent gesture of pride, instead of its actual use as a symbol for persecution. Tragically, the boy was deported the following year to Auschwitz, where he was murdered along with about 1,500 Jews of Rhodes. Photo from Miru Alcana.

Source: Rhodes Historical Foundation

July 1944: the Jews of Rhodes were detained at the Air Force Command center located just outside the Old City near the Gate of Amboise. The Jews were held there for 3 days prior to their deportation to Auschwitz.

Source: Rhodes Historical Foundation

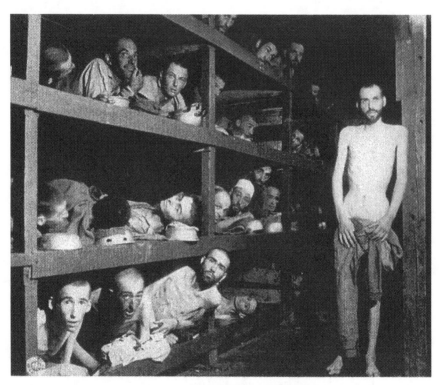

U.S. Military Archives photos ordered to be kept by Allied Supreme Commander
General Dwight D. Eisenhower

*U.S. Military Archives photos ordered to be kept by Allied Supreme Commander
General Dwight D. Eisenhower*

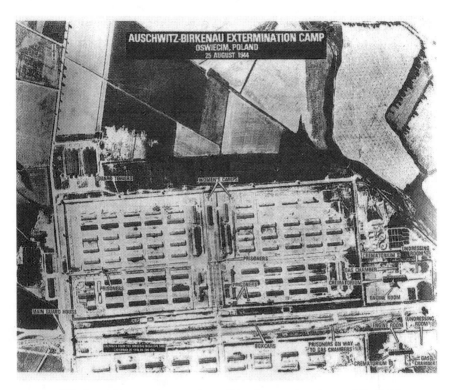

Allied aerial reconnaissance photo of Auschwitz taken August 25th 1944

This is a file from the Wikimedia Commons. *The description on its description page there is shown below.*

Commons is a freely licensed media file repository. This artistic work created by the United Kingdom Government is in the public domain

1946 photo of the President of the Jewish Community, Elia Soriano, laying a wreath at the fountain in "La Juderia" in memory of the Jewish victims of the Holocaust. Photo from Elie Jacob Soriano.

Source: Rhodes Historical Foundation

1946 photo of ten young Rhodesli men survivors of the Nazi concentration camps. The photo was taken in Ostia, Italy (near Rome) where the refugees lived in temporary housing. (The Rhodesli women were housed in a shelter in Rome.) Left to right: Alberto Levy, Jack Hasson, Victor Hasson, Samuel "Samy" Modiano, Eliezer Sourmani, Pepo Cordoval, Jack Cordoval, Joseph Conae, Ner Alhadeff and Joseph Hasson.

Photo Source: Rhodes Historical Foundation

June 1945 photo in Bologna, Italy of six young Rhodesli women survivors of the concentration camps. They were liberated one month earlier and traveled by train to Italy. In Bologna they met at a military barracks with British soldiers of the Jewish Brigade from Palestine.

Photo Source: Rhodes Historical Foundation

The Holocaust Memorial was erected in the "Square of the Martyred Jews." The dedication on a six-sided black granite column is in memory of the World War Two victims from Rhodes and the island of Cos. Each of the sides is inscribed in a different language: Greek, Hebrew, English, French, Italian and Judeo-Spanish ("Ladino"). The memorial is inscribed with the words: "IN ETERNAL MEMORY OF THE 1604 JEWISH MARTYRS OF RHODES AND COS WHO WERE MURDERED IN NAZI DEATH CAMPS. JULY 23, 1944."

Photo Source: Isaac Benatar August, 2007

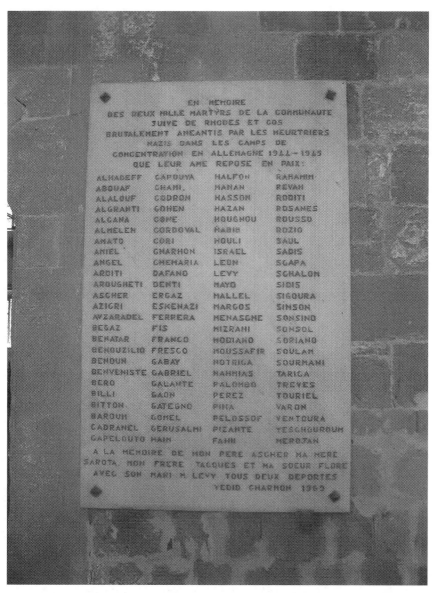

EN MEMOIRE
DES DEUX MILLE MARTYRS DE LA COMMUNAUTE
JUIVE DE RHODES ET COS
BRUTALEMENT ANEANTIS PAR LES MEURTRIERS
NAZIS DANS LES CAMPS DE
CONCENTRATION EN ALLEMAGNE 1944-1945
QUE LEUR AME REPOSE EN PAIX

ALHADEFF	CAPOUYA	HALFON	RAHAMIM
ABOUAF	CHAMI,	HANAN	REVAH
ALALOUF	CODRON	HASSON	RODITI
ALGRANTI	COHEN	HAZAN	ROSANES
ALCANA	COPE	HOUGNOU	ROUSSO
ALMELEH	CORDOVAL	HABIB	ROZIO
AMATO	CORI	HOULI	SAUL
ANIEL	CHARHON	ISRAEL	SADIS
ANGEL	CHEMARIA	LEON	SOAPA
ARDITI	DAFANO	LEVY	SCHALON
AROUGHETI	DENTI	MAYO	SIDIS
ASCHER	ERGAZ	MALLEL	SIGOURA
AZIGRI	ESKENAZI	MARGOS	SIMSON
AVZARADEL	FERRERA	MENASCHE	SONSINO
BEGAZ	FIS	MIZRAHI	SOMSOL
BENATAR	FRANCO	MODIANO	SORIANO
BENOUZILIO	FRESCO	MOUSSAFIR	SOULAM
BEHOUN	GABAY	MOTRIGA	SOURMAMI
BENVENISTE	GABRIEL	NAHMIAS	TARICA
BERO	GALANTE	PALOMBO	TREVES
BILLI	GAON	PEREZ	TOURIEL
BITTON,	GATEGNO	PINA	VARON
BAROUH	GOMEL	PELOSSOF	VENTOURA
CADRANEL	GERUSALMI	PIZANTE	YESCHOUROUM
CAPELOUTO	HAIM	FAHN	MEROJAN

A LA MEMOIRE DE MON PERE ASCHER MA MERE
SAROTA MON FRERE TACQUES ET MA SOEUR FLORE
AVEC SON MARI M LEVY TOUS DEUX DEPORTES
YEDID CHARHON 1969

Plaque outside the entrance to the Kahal Shalom Synagogue containing the family names of those taken by the Nazis to the concentration camps

Photo source: Isaac Benatar

View from the gallery of the inside of the Kahal Shalom Synagogue as it looks today
Photo Source; Isaac Benatar

Holocaust survivor, Samy (left), with Author (right), at the Kahal Shalom Synagogue, Rhodes Island September 2007.

Photo Source: Isaac Benatar

Several hundred year old Torah kept secreted in the Morad Reis Mosque during World War Two; on display at the Kahal Shalom Rhodes Historical Museum. Rhodes Island

Photo Source: Isaac Benatar